COUSTEAU'S PAPUA NEW GUINEA JOURNEY

COUSTEAU'S PAPUA NEW GUINEA JOURNEY

Jean-Michel Cousteau
and Mose Richards

HARRY N. ABRAMS, INC.
PUBLISHERS, NEW YORK

Editor: Robert Morton
Designer: Elissa Ichiyasu
Photo research: Anne-Marie Cousteau
Scientific consultant: Dr. Richard C. Murphy
Publication coordinator: Lesley D. High

The Cousteau Society wishes to express its gratitude
to Ted Turner and Robert Wussler, whose support made
possible the expedition chronicled in this book.

Library of Congress Cataloging-in-Publication Data
Cousteau, Jean-Michel.
Jacques Cousteau's journey to Papua New Guinea
by Jean-Michel Cousteau and Mose Richards.
p.   cm.
ISBN 0-8109-3151-6
1. Papua New Guinea—Description and travel.
2. Cousteau, Jacques Yves—Journeys—Papua New Guinea.
3. Ethnology—Papua New Guinea.
4. Natural history—Papua New Guinea.
I. Richards, Mose.
II. Title.
DU740.2.C68 1989
919.5′3—dc19   89–317

BOMC offers recordings and compact discs, cassettes
and records. For information and catalog write to
BOMR, Camp Hill, PA 17012.

CONTENTS

SHARING BUBBLES

Once upon a time, in northern Los Angeles, I paid a visit to my elder son, Jean-Michel, who had just settled into a new home with his wife Anne-Marie and my two grandchildren. The house was not easy to find, tucked into a maze of narrow winding roads and hidden behind a curtain of vigorous trees. On the gate, etched in a brass plate, was an exotic name: "WUVULU". A dachshund named Cuscus barked at my heels. Anne-Marie, with two-year-old Celine, was preparing tea while Fabien was blowing his proud seven years in large soap bubbles.

Jean-Michel told me all about Wuvulu, a coral island north of Papua New Guinea, where he had organized educational vacations for groups of ecologically-minded citizens of all ages and from all walks of life. He had fallen in love with Wuvulu, its native inhabitants, and the exuberant local marine fauna. He described the beauty of the reefs, the crowd of rodent sharks, and the frequent incursions of a family of impressive orcas.

In all my adventures as a nomad of the sea, I had never visited that part of the world. For once, I was the one to marvel at someone else's adventures, and that someone was my son. Jean-Michel was happy to return to me the bedazzlement he had so often shared in the wake of early *Calypso* voyages. And I was proud that my son was now able to fill me with wonder. We swore that, sooner or later, we would both share the excitement of exploring Papua New Guinea and the surrounding Bismarck Sea.

Years passed. Finally, our dream came true. On board *Calypso*, I joined Jean-Michel and our windship *Alcyone* for one of our most fascinating expeditions. The book I introduce today is the fruit of our mutual love for the Sea, for Nature, and for People.

The passion for color and ceremony in Papua New Guinea is amply demonstrated by Highland village women, who create costumes for a ritual celebration out of natural elements—feathers, shells, pigments, foliage, and marsupial skins.

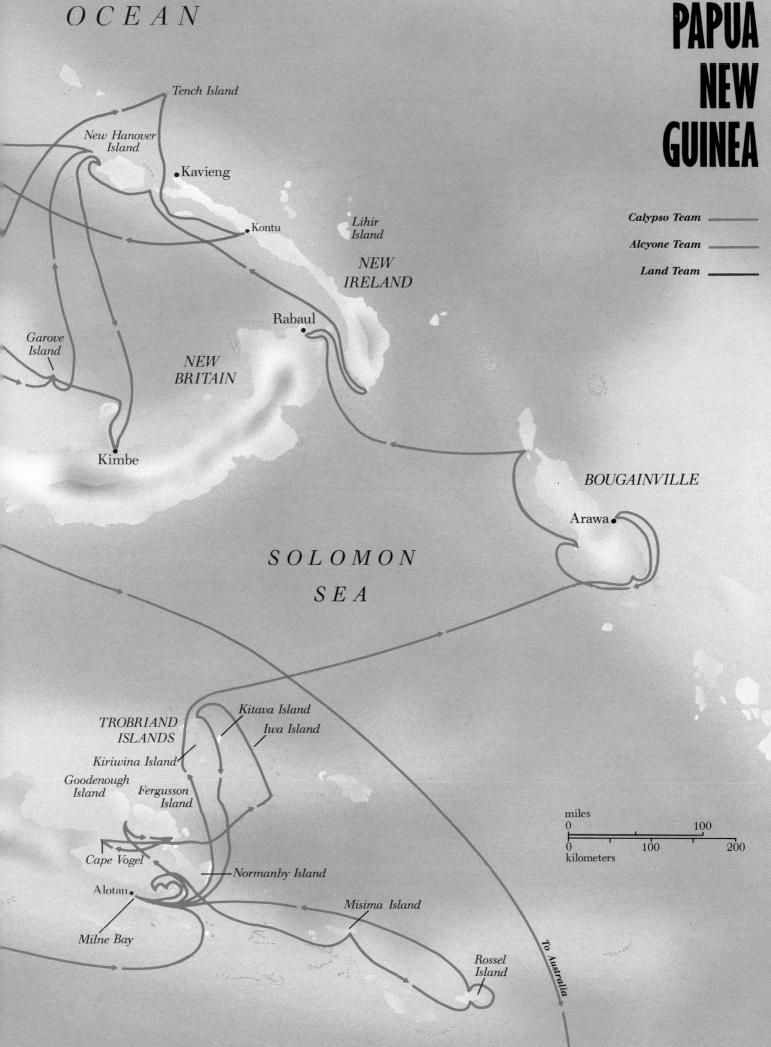

OCEAN

PAPUA NEW GUINEA

Calypso Team
Alcyone Team
Land Team

Tench Island

New Hanover Island

Kavieng

Kontu

Lihir Island

NEW IRELAND

Rabaul

Garove Island

NEW BRITAIN

Kimbe

BOUGAINVILLE

Arawa

SOLOMON SEA

Kitava Island

TROBRIAND ISLANDS

Iwa Island

Kiriwina Island

Goodenough Island

Fergusson Island

Cape Vogel

Normanby Island

Alotau

Misima Island

Milne Bay

To Australia

Rossel Island

miles
0   100
0   100   200
kilometers

INTO THE TIME MACHINE

Every beginning

is a consequence—

every beginning

ends something.

Paul Valery

A view of Highland valleys near Bulolo reveals the ruggedness of Papua New Guinea's interior terrain. But for the gravel road, the scene probably resembles the vista that greeted the first outsiders who trekked here in search of gold.

On the morning of May 27, 1930, shortly after dawn, an event took place that can never happen again on earth. Two gold prospectors from Australia and fifteen native carriers walked into a Highland valley of what is now Papua New Guinea and discovered to their astonishment a previously unknown civilization of nearly one million people who had never before had contact with the outside world. It was the beginning of the last epic encounter between the globe-conquering, technological society of the West and a culture not profoundly changed since the Stone Age.

The men and women who swarmed about Michael Leahy and Michael Dwyer had never seen white skin before. They had never seen a wheel. They carried bows and arrows and stone axes. An old man touched Leahy to see if he was real, then rubbed his bare legs to see if they were painted. Some of the women wept joyfully, hugging one another. They assumed that the two pale figures in khaki shorts and fedora hats were ancestral spirits returned from the dead.

Perhaps the most remarkable aspect of this startling confrontation was that it did not occur until more than four hundred years after the discovery of New Guinea by European explorers. Such a large civilization could remain undetected for so long because it reposed in seclusion within a great bulwark of nature. Perhaps no place of comparable size on the planet is so difficult to penetrate. Across an expanse larger than either California or Sweden stretches a landscape buckled by steep mountain slopes, matted with dense jungle, engulfed in vast swamps. Because the island is among earth's most daunting settings, because the equatorial heat and monsoonal humidity and tropical diseases can swiftly discourage visitors, and because there was no evidence until quite recently of great mineral riches to be carried away, New Guinea was the last inhabited region on the planet to be explored by Europeans.

The past half century has brought slow but inevitable change, yet throughout the main island and among the confetti of six hundred smaller islands off its shores, great pockets of antiquity endure. There are people who have had only the vaguest contact with the modern world. There are tracts of rain forest still unsurveyed by terrestrial biologists, and seas that remain largely unknown to marine science. Moreover, these natural habitats are thought to be among the richest and most diverse remaining on the planet.

Triggered by discoveries of immense mineral wealth and by the escalating encroachment of twentieth century materialism, a great temblor of fundamental change is striking today. Parts of the society are springing elastically from primordial times to the Space Age in the span of a single generation, even a single young life. The convulsions begin only now to ripple through the world views of curious millions, some still adorned in feathers and shells, and through the natural worlds around them, through the jungle canopy, the rope-brown rivers, the encircling sea. Yet, while other peoples in other lands grapple with the problems of irreparably diminished or contaminated worlds, the long isolation of New Guinea has left it mostly intact, mostly wild, mostly salvable.

There may be a better opportunity to spare invaluable surviving pieces of the human and environmental past here than anywhere else on the planet, and an opportunity to blend in a future society what is worthy from ancient times and what enriches modern life. These exhilarating possibilities can occur only if they are recognized now, and if the appropriate attention is given the preservable riches, and if sufficient support is extended to those in Papua New Guinea who would save them.

A young man perches among trees at the edge of the village of Walya near Mount Hagen.

Prop roots splayed out from the trunk of a pandanus palm allow the tree to remain upright even in soggy soils. The many species of pandanus are among Papua New Guinea's most important forest resources, providing villagers with timber and firewood, leaves for thatching and weaving, and nuts valued as a common food.

Within the next few years, elements of life known to a hundred generations will be swept away in the engulfing wave of new gadgets and mobilities and possibilities. Not all of the losses will be lamentable. Among the ways of life jettisoned into time will be measures of daily pain and suffering. There will be less keening in the night over the deaths of children. Fewer lungs will be destroyed by the smokepots meant to drive mosquitoes from a hut through the night. The great society-wide trick will be to keep that which is precious and dignifying while discarding that which is merely tedious, or mostly dangerous.

In Papua New Guinea, it is a heroic moment and a time of pathos. It is a period of infinite opportunity, or of shattering loss, or both.

To witness this titanic battle between what once was and what could be, Jacques and Jean-Michel Cousteau began organizing a formidable expedition in 1988 that would take two ships, two aircraft, several four-wheel-drive vehicles, and three teams composed of divers, scientists, sailors, and filmmakers throughout much of Papua New Guinea. One goal was to preserve on film for posterity a record of this historic time, and of living tribes and creatures that may ultimately vanish. Another goal was to help bring scientific analysis to bear on the management of the country's rich and diverse natural resources, to provide information to the navigators of Papua New Guinea's destiny that might enable them to save their habitats and cultures from wholesale deterioration as new ideas and technologies burst in from the outside world.

The 1,500-mile-long island of New Guinea is the world's largest tropical island, second only to Greenland as the largest island on earth. It is a plot of land as large as France and Germany combined. The independent nation called Papua New Guinea occupies the eastern half of New Guinea. The western half, called Irian Jaya, has been a part of the Republic of Indonesia since 1963. Since relations have not always been cordial between the two political entities governing New Guinea, the Cousteau mission would be limited to the eastern half.

Though Irian Jaya's environment is similar, Papua New Guinea holds a greater fascination for most of the world because its peoples and their artwork are cloaked in legend, because its offshore islands conjure up images of Eden, because pivotal battles of World War II were fought across its lands and seas, and because it is suddenly quaking with change.

The notion of mounting a major expedition to explore Papua New Guinea had tantalized Jean-Michel Cousteau for fifteen years. With marine biologist Dr. Richard Murphy he had conducted underwater surveys over the years at tiny Wuvulu Island in the Bismarck Sea, which lies off the north coast. Divers since childhood, both men were electrified by the aquatic spectacles they encountered: vast shoals of reef fish drifting across coral heads, swimmers and bottom-dwellers alike emblazoned with dazzling hues; white-tip sharks patrolling lazily by day, stalking by night; venomous creatures like the blue-ringed octopus clutching the sea floor; harmless nomads like the manta ray gliding on delta wings through a bluewater sky.

Though their contact with the interior of the country and its cultures had been limited, both had followed the events of the country from afar. Now, as The Cousteau Society ventured into the Pacific as part of its globe-circling project called "Cousteau's Rediscovery of the World," an expedition to Papua New Guinea became possible. Following two separate courses around the world, *Calypso* would reach New Caledonia in the winter of 1987–88, and the new Turbosail windship *Alcyone* would arrive in Guam. The Cousteaus decided that both ships would rendezvous in Papua New Guinea, their first meeting since the vessels joined to sail into New York harbor nearly three years earlier, marking the successful completion of *Alcyone*'s experimental transatlantic maiden voyage.

In Los Angeles, Murphy and Cousteau researcher Neal Shapiro began compiling an immense fact and contact book that would guide water and land teams. A more urgent task, however, was the initiation of the process of obtaining permissions for the expedition from the government of Papua New Guinea. Shapiro quickly learned that it can take six to eight months to secure the requisite papers of entry, far longer than in most countries. In part, this is a result of Papua New Guinea's relatively recent entry into the business of managing a bureaucracy. A history of colonial rule by Holland, Britain, Germany, and Australia ended only in 1975, when Australia granted independence.

At the beginning of January, worried that the expedition would be delayed, the Cousteaus sent Society logistics coordinator Karen Brazeau to Port Moresby, the nation's capital, to prepare the complex arrangements that would permit ships, aircraft, and crews to enter and to probe the country. Born in Canada, Brazeau has worked with the Cousteaus for nearly fifteen years, as an administrator in their Monaco and New York offices, and as the chief support person on expeditions from Canada to the South Pacific.

The advance logistics job is one of the most difficult on an expedition. Every person and every piece of equipment that moves into a country must be cleared in advance, transported about within the country according to government regulations as well as expedition schedules and routes, and ultimately accounted for as teams depart the country. Every step involves filling out and filing forms, visiting bureaucrats and ships' handlers and ticket agents and banks, and making the flurry of telephone calls that inevitably precedes and follows every action. Though she is based in New York City, Brazeau had been traveling constantly for months to handle details of *Calypso*'s previous missions in Tahiti and the Tuamotos Islands and in Australia. By the time she could leave Papua New Guinea—the last Cousteau person out—she would have spent a full year away from home.

Brazeau takes up residence, first in a guest house in Port Moresby, then in the Islander Hotel in Boroko, a suburb of the capital that houses most of the national government and is located midway between downtown Moresby, where commerce is centered, and Jackson Airport, where she will be spending considerable time nearly every day. She opens an office in the Islander, which becomes the headquarters and staging area.

Six weeks later, French cinematographer Jean-Paul Cornu and researcher Neal Shapiro arrive in Moresby. Shapiro has in hand the research "bible" prepared in Los Angeles. Cornu has spent considerable time in Paris libraries studying the culture and history of Papua New Guinea. Now, to formulate a filming plan for the Highlands region, the two men spend fifteen-hour workdays at the Islander sharing information and constructing a huge map of the country, with colored dots representing points of interest for the expedition. Concerned by all they have read about the sometimes violent cultures of the interior, they produce an advisory to be read by all Cousteau personnel who enter the country:

TRAVEL WARNINGS: If you are involved in or see an accident while driving, do NOT stop; continue to the nearest police station and report it. If you hit a pig, do

NOT stop but proceed immediately to the nearest police station. If while driving you see people walking with axes, knives, or bows and arrows, do NOT stop. Keep moving. If you come to a barrier across a road, turn around.

In Moresby, the Cousteau advance team learns through the daily papers of a crime wave plaguing the capital city. Gangs of impoverished young men, locally called rascals, are said to be everywhere, especially at night. Sensational stories of murders, rapes, and robberies fill the newspapers. Conjecture over the cause of the violence leads to several theories—the frustration of urban poor who have migrated from the countryside and cannot find work, the residue of Highlands cultural violence, the resistance to central authority rooted in the country's entire history.

Yet the team finds an endearing charm and sophistication among the professional people of the capital. A local couple who have befriended Brazeau, Joan and Keli Taureka, treat the team to a *mumu*, the tropical equivalent of a western backyard barbecue in which the meal is traditionally baked in banana leaves in an underground pit. The couple also helps the team grow familiar with Pidgin, the mixture of Melanesian dialects and English that has evolved for centuries and now represents a lingua franca among the less-well-educated in Papua New Guinea society. It is common for educated natives of the country to speak three languages fluently: their tribal tongue, Pidgin, and English, which is the official language.

Though a legitimate and respected language, Pidgin can sound amusing to newcomers. If something is broken, it has *gone bagarap*. A helicopter is a *Mixmaster bilong Jesus Christ*. Prince Charles of Britain is *Nambawan Son bilong Misus Kwin*. I am thirsty: *Nek bilong mi drai*. To kill someone is: *Kilim i dai pinis* (Kill him he die finish). Twin syllable words are common: a white foreigner is a *dimdim*, food is *kaikai*, human waste is *pekpek*, small is *liklik*, a crocodile is a *pukpuk*, a mosquito is a *natnat*. A restaurant is a *haus kaikai*, a bathroom is a *haus pekpek*. Breakfast is *kaikai bilong moningtem*. Hair is *gras bilong het*. Perhaps the most inspired invention of the language, however, is the Pidgin for piano: *Bigfella bockus, teeth alla same shark, you hitim he cry out*.

A week after the arrival of Cornu and Shapiro, the advance party is completed with the addition of expedition science director Dick Murphy, and director of still photography Anne-Marie Cousteau. It is now only days before *Calypso* is expected to arrive in Port Moresby ready to work, and the mandatory authorizations and visas have not yet been supplied by the government's Department of Foreign Affairs.

Meanwhile, Captain Cousteau in Paris and Jean-Michel—traveling between Los Angeles, New York, and Paris—are in daily communication to make crew assignments and to finalize the overall expedition plan.

J.-M. C.: Only two previous expeditions—to the Antarctic and the Amazon—have evoked the odd mixture of exhilaration and dread I have experienced as we contemplate sending friends and equipment into Papua New Guinea. The characteristics that made these two realms fascinating to us also made them enormously difficult to explore, and occasionally dangerous. Papua New Guinea, though not as vast as the others, presents the same general obstacles. In remoteness, one uncovers surprises that illuminate life's array of wonders, but one also loses the communication and transportation lines that could be vital in the event of an emergency.

In Papua New Guinea, we enter waters that have been precisely charted only along the established sailing routes and along mainland coasts. In a similar situation two years earlier, following a navigational chart spotted with areas of unknown depths and hazards, Alcyone struck a submerged rock near Cape Horn. Though we in the crew were not gravely endangered since the shore was close by, our new windship was in great danger of sinking. It took twenty-four hours before help arrived from the Chilean Navy, during which time we were dependent on the continuous operation of our two water-evacuating pumps.

We will also face tropical diseases, primarily malaria. Our research indicates that one strain of this mosquito-borne malady in Papua New Guinea is resistant so far to all preventative drugs, and is potentially lethal.

There is a constant worry, also, about the safety of our teams during the hundreds of hours they will be airborne in our Cousteau Society amphibious plane and in our two-man helicopter. The sparcity of roads in Papua New Guinea and the considerable distances we must cross—over mainland mountains and jungle and across empty stretches of sea—will make us more reliant on air transport than during most expeditions. Yet the climate of Papua New Guinea can make flying treacherous. The term "rocky clouds" is common among pilots who fly here, since thunderheads routinely cover the country's central peaks, some of which rival the Alps in height. And sudden storms can speedily surround a small plane during a water crossing, making it nearly impossible to find the destination, often just a tiny atoll in the trackless sea.

I think of my few previous flights across Papua New Guinea over the years, and the bare facts in our research turn into vivid images. One looks across a green cloak of tree canopy similar to that of the Amazon—rough-textured, mottled, dense; but here it is folded and creased everywhere. There are bladelike ridges and knobs that slope abruptly into shadowy pockets or plunging gorges. The land seems bunched up into a phalanx of hills and mountains. There are few holes in the green fur, but even where the canopy breaks, the skin beneath is bright green.

In the north, adjacent to the mighty Sepik River—a serpentine giant navigable three hundred miles upstream—the landscape changes suddenly. Rain forest gives way to a flat, grassy savannah. The jungle contracts into wide belts that meander like black-green rivers across a vast lawn. Flying, one comes upon a village, set just inside the jungle belt. Soon another, situated like the first, and then the realization that they are a string of villages, each about ten miles apart. They are quiet; smokeless and absent movement if it is midmorning or afternoon, smudged with haze and alive with moving figures if it is mealtime.

Offshore, one looks down upon endless tracts of the scalloped, cobalt-blue sea surface, sometimes for hours before coming to turquoise-rimmed islands. Like the mainland, they are mostly blanketed with trees. Some are flat, limestone platforms, some are volcanic peaks. Circling over the shallows at the edge of an island, one can find an occasional undersea cloud, which turns out to be a fish school. On one flight I watched a shark dash in and out of a shoal of small fish. On another, five dugongs turned their heads toward us, then quickly dived out of sight.

Skirting the coast of an island, one sees village clearings much like those in the mainland interior, but here the adjacent surf is inevitably full of children, for whom the ocean is a playground. An entire day can be whiled away chasing crabs or fingerling fish in the shallows—the "toys" nature bestows on youngsters growing up in a tropical wilderness.

More than seven hundred tribes dwell in these various settings within the Papua New Guinea boundaries. Across millennia, they have remained so re-

Photographed off Wuvulu Island, a soft coral illustrates the beauty and intricacy of reef organisms. Soft corals, which belong to the class of coelenterates known as anthozoa, do not contribute to reef building as do hard corals. Their trunklike spicules—slender calcareous structures—support flexible branches instead of solid masses. They provide habitats for a variety of reef dwellers.

Like modern urban dwellers, soft corals (*Sarcophyton*) photographed at Wuvulu Island construct vertical projections that increase available living space. Each white spot is an individual coral polyp.

Largest among Papua New Guinea's marsupials, tree kangaroos offer living evidence of the ancient land bridge that connected the country to Australia some fifteen million years ago. As many as six species of tree kangaroos survive in Papua New Guinea, while only two species can still be found in Australia.

mote from one another, for the most part, that they developed and still speak more than seven hundred languages, estimated by some experts to represent nearly half of all the languages in the world. Though the present population of about three and a half million is the largest of any South Pacific island group, most people still live in rural settings.

The environment, like the cultures embedded within it, is unique. Papua New Guinea is a biological crossroads, where species from Australia and Asia mingle, and where this evolutionary mixture across eons has produced creatures found nowhere else, some of extraordinary form or behavior. There are thirty-seven species of birds of paradise here, and only six in the rest of the world. There are flightless cassowaries and tree-dwelling kangaroos. There are more than seventy species of snakes. There are rare butterflies flitting among equally rare orchids. The undersea world, too, teems with curiosities and beauties, with giant tridacna clams, with deep-dwelling chambered nautilus, with lobsters that queue up and march off in seasonal migrations that remain a mystery to science. The marine environment, of course, is even less known than the terrestrial rain forests.

As we contemplate a survey of Papua New Guinea, we realize an uncommon opportunity lies before us: to peer into and to document a province of the sea uniquely undistorted by the modern world, and a people perhaps still as intimately in touch with their natural surroundings as our earliest forebears.

The paramount questions we hope to answer through our work are: how much of the natural world still remains pristine? And how much of the human culture has been altered by outside contact? Our chief scientist, Dick Murphy, hopes to provide new scientific information to the government of Papua New Guinea as a result of the mission. He has arranged for a broad analysis of the country's resource use and environmental base by a team of scientists from the University of Florida, headed by Dr. H. T. Odum. The same team has conducted similar studies of the Amazon, Mississippi, and Sea of Cortez in association with The Cousteau Society, and their report will offer a new technique and model enabling Papua New Guinea to work toward a higher standard of living without depleting its rich natural heritage. Hopefully, our constructive suggestions will help the nation avoid the errors of other developing countries, where vital and renewable resources for future generations have been sacrificed for short-term advances in the standard of living.

A spectacular pair of birds of paradise display their art for an as yet uninterested female of the species. (Photograph by David Gillison)

My father and I decide to organize three teams for the expedition. **Calypso's** *crew, led by Captain Albert Falco, will explore the islands scattered about Papua New Guinea. A Land Team, composed of only six or seven people, will penetrate the interior Highlands in rugged vehicles. And* **Alcyone's** *crew will sail up the Sepik River, then remain after the departure of the other teams to finish uncompleted studies. My father and I will shuttle between the various teams to direct important missions, relying on our amphibious plane* **Papagallo** *— christened in the Amazon — to act as a wilderness taxi and equipment-moving pickup. If all works well, we will return from Papua New Guinea with data for evaluating its future, and with film that will preserve forever the exotic images still visible through the human and environmental time machine of this faraway paradise.*

But in Port Moresby, as the appointed arrival time of *Calypso* nears, the required papers permitting entry of ship and crew into Papua New Guinea have still not been forthcoming from government authorities. As the advance team frets over this dilemma, Karen Brazeau discovers what may be the source of the delay. Sources in the capital tell her that a French filmmaker has recently produced a program about the nation that has inflamed emotions here. The film is said to portray the country as barbaric, and the leadership that has guided it since independence from Australia

At Misima Island in Milne Bay land is cleared for a new gold mine project. Cultural and economic upheaval triggered by mining in many parts of Papua New Guinea have begun to strain the social fabric and to threaten a delicate ecology. On Misima, two generations of islanders have come in conflict over compensation agreements for the use of their land — the young protest that their parents settled for too little money.

in 1975 as incompetent. Now, in the wake of treatment they consider slanderous at the hands of a French producer, the authorities are being petitioned by a cinema team that is largely French, aboard French-flag vessels, to make an even more ambitious film. Moreover, the name Cousteau is not familiar to most people in Papua New Guinea, since Cousteau programs are not shown on local television. It becomes clear that suspicions about the expedition and its motives are causing an internal debate in the government. The arrival of the Cousteau team comes at an unfortunate time. Violence has broken out in nearby New Caledonia between the French colonial government and revolutionary islanders called Kanaks. The government of Papua New Guinea is pro-Kanak and, by extension, anti-French.

One remedy has been to emphasize the American nature of the team. Many individuals are from the U.S.; The Cousteau Society is based in the U.S.; and the funding organization, Turner Broadcasting, is American. But suspicions linger. To further allay fears, Brazeau and Murphy send out a blanket invitation among government officials to a film screening at the Islander Hotel of "Journey to a Thousand Rivers," the first installment of Cousteau's Peabody Award–winning Amazon series. The film, portraying a hauntingly beautiful world and a dignified people, is warmly received. "That's the kind of work we do," the two Cousteau veterans tell the audience, "and that's the kind of film series we'll produce about your country." To the astonishment of Brazeau and Murphy, the complete packet of delayed visas is issued the next day.

By the end of the first week of March, the members of the Land Team have arrived in Moresby. Cornu, who has developed a detailed plan for the Highlands mission, is eager to get started filming. Anne-Marie Cousteau, a still photographer and veteran of Cousteau expeditions throughout the world who happens also to be Jean-Michel's wife, and Expedition Leader Don Santee, a veteran diver based in the Los Angeles office of The Cousteau Society, will share responsibilities with Cornu for the land mission. The team is completed by sound engineer Gary Holland, diver Marc Blessington, and a local camera apprentice, Martin Medan, who will act as an assistant cameraman and translator.

On March 7th, the Land Team fly to the northeastern port city of Lae, where they lease two four-wheel-drive station wagons and set out for the Highlands.

Meanwhile, a few days in advance of *Calypso*, the amphibious float plane *Papagallo* arrives in Port Moresby from a mission in Australia. Dick Murphy, who has been eager to make reconnaissance trips along the itinerary being developed for *Calypso*, now has access to the mobility he needs. The plan is for Brazeau and Shapiro to remain in Port Moresby to handle the myriad details of logistics, while Murphy in *Papagallo*— flown initially by Alaskan bush pilot Bill Kalbrener—scouts locations and notifies local authorities of the crew's proposed work along the ship's route.

The Cousteau biologist—one of the most experienced divers on the staff—will search out local people who can direct him to underwater sites of sufficient interest to the film crew. More importantly, he will try to find and to explain the team's objectives to the local "big men," the chiefs and priests and provincial officials whose power it is to welcome visitors or to turn them away.

As the Cousteau team will learn in greater detail through the coming months, the authority of the central government can be usurped by a provincial office, and the authority of both the federal and provincial officials can be completely ignored at the whim of a chief in a distant village. The same local independence that has given rise to more than seven hundred languages can produce nearly as many different responses to outsiders seeking entry to islands, villages, or even offshore waters.

Almost immediately, on the North Solomon island of Bougainville, Murphy encounters a wall of distrust. The Provincial Secretary expresses what will become a common reaction among local authorities to the arrival of a foreign film team: If we allow you to benefit by taking away images of our world, he wonders, what do our villagers gain? The widespread opinion is that anthropologists, filmmakers, and others have used Papua New Guinea to establish their own fame and fortune, while leaving nothing behind to the subjects of their work.

Murphy explains that The Cousteau Society intends to provide information and expertise from the developed world that will help Papua New Guinea make critical scientific and resource-management decisions. The Cousteau films produced here, he says, will introduce the nation and people to hundreds of millions of viewers around the world, and will do so in an accurate and sensitive way.

The Provincial Secretary remains unconvinced. Now worried, since the entire expedition could be in jeopardy if local authorities are similarly recalcitrant, Murphy gives a video cassette of "Journey to a Thousand Rivers" to the Secretary and leaves. Returning the next day to continue the difficult negotiation, Murphy learns that the Secretary viewed the film, then played it for his children, then invited the neighbors over. The suspicions have evaporated. Permission is granted.

Over the course of the next few weeks, with Kalbrener acting as an airborne chauffeur, Murphy follows an exhausting schedule from island to island, rushing from small airports or grass airstrips to hurried meetings, dashing out to reconnoiter the landscape in rented cars, diving whenever possible to check out potential underwater filming locations, catching a few hours sleep in small hotels or huts, then setting off again.

Murphy, Kalbrener, and local guide and translator Telita Halstead are also the first to experience the trials of flight in Papua New Guinea. On a trip in *Papagallo* from the mainland to Goodenough and Fergusson islands, they are suddenly encompassed by a severe storm. Visibility drops

In the humid rain forests of Papua New Guinea, abundant mosses and lichens (like those pictured here) help break down dead vegetation and speed the process of recycling nutrients and regenerating life.

Hibiscus blossoms are found throughout Papua New Guinea, providing colorful decorations for villagers, who commonly wear the flowers in their hair.

to zero as they penetrate the surrounding clouds. Fearful of flying into one of the peaks on the two islands ahead, Kalbrener decides to set down on the ocean and wait out the storm.

Peering out the windows of the seaplane, the three gaze at a featureless world of gray—gray clouds above, gray mists veiling the horizons about them, and swells of gray water rocking them from below. It is an eerie and lonely scene, accompanied by the steady percussion of rain on the cowling and seawater lapping against the floats. When the storm has continued unabated for more than an hour, with no signs it will soon pass, the three decide to abort their trip. Kalbrener takes off and flies by instruments back to the mainland, returning safely over open water.

There are, as well, vexations less dramatic but more frequent. Like most of the tropical world, Papua New Guinea supports a vast and varied population of small organisms—from bacteria to insects and spiders. With a fervent interest in all manifestations of biology, Murphy relishes the opportunity to observe carnivorous centipedes and decayed-vegetation-consuming millipedes, and to photograph a praying mantis clinging to a pandanus tree. Where others might be repelled by the arrival of ants or cockroaches on the table of a local restaurant, or a blizzard of moths circling the light overhead, Murphy finds exhilaration in such events, seizing the opportunity to conduct experiments where possible. What is the defensive behavior of the ants trekking across the tablecloth? Murphy threatens with a toothpick. They raise their abdomens, but bite rather than sting. Murphy makes a mental note.

Yet even the inveterate biologist can find the hordes of insects unsettling at times. Since his days in the Amazon, Murphy has carried with him a flashlight that is mounted on a headband. The gadget is handy when one seeks to read in a tent or in a remote hotel without electricity. While spending a night in a Catholic mission on Rossel Island, Murphy tries to catch up on his reading of articles about Papua New Guinea, using the illumination supplied by a moth-engulfed bare bulb hanging from the ceiling. When the mission generator is turned off for the night and the bulb goes out, he dons his headband light. Promptly, the cloud of moths swarms from the darkened bulb to the light on Murphy's forehead, making it impossible to read as the frenzied mass thrashes about his eyes, nose, and mouth.

As the weeks pass, an array of insect bites over much of Murphy's body blossoms into welts and open sores. The scientist is the first to experience some of the health menaces that will later plague the crew members of all three Cousteau teams.

On March 18, *Calypso* at last enters Port Moresby. Because the ship has been delayed in leaving New Caledonia by mechanical problems—a large chunk of carbon and salt blocking the fresh water in the exhaust manifold water jacket, a problem that took four days of engine dismantling to find—the crew is anxious to set off on their mission as soon as possible. After one day of replenishment and diplomacy, *Calypso* sails eastward to Alotau, the capital of Milne Bay Province. En route, Murphy leads a briefing on the bridge among those with key responsibilities: Captain Falco, shipboard director of cinematography Louis Prezelin, helicopter pilot Bob Braunbeck, chief diver Bertrand Sion, second cameraman Chuck Davis, and sound engineer Yves Zlotnicka.

An orb weaver spider fashions a web that is elegant to the human eye yet a lethal snare for passing insects. Wavy designs radiating from the center are a signature pattern of orb weavers, perhaps employed to confuse their predators.

Among the most exotic of Papua New Guinea's rain-forest insects, the vegetarian walking stick has been shaped by evolution to resemble a twig, an effective camouflage protecting it from predators.

What appears to be a living insect is, in fact, the empty exoskeleton of a cicada, left behind when the creature molted. Larvae spend up to two years living underground, then emerge to mate, lay eggs on twigs, and die. Using membranes in the thorax, male cicadas produce the loudest noises of all insects.

As the ship approaches Alotau on the 20th, Murphy and Prezelin speed ahead in a Zodiac to meet the Premier of Milne Bay Province, Navy Aule, and to inform him that the expedition is ready to proceed. In a provincial headquarters reminiscent of a World War II Quonset hut, they are greeted warmly by the Premier, but told that his Science Committee must approve their plans. Believing that the obligatory authorization had already been arranged, the two visitors grow nervous. Offshore, twenty-eight people in a ship outfitted with a helicopter, a submarine, and elaborate diving equipment are ready to begin a journey that could suddenly be cancelled.

Thinking quickly, the two Cousteau leaders invite the Premier and his Science Committee to a luncheon aboard *Calypso*, and a tour of the vessel. All goes well, but the permission is not yet granted. Back to the dock in Alotau, and into an automobile for the short return trip to provincial headquarters. The driver switches on his car radio. As Prezelin and Murphy gaze out at the lush tropical scenes surrounding the town, feeling the hot air and humidity streaming in the open windows, they hear through booming speakers a recording of carolers singing "Oh Come, All Ye Faithful," complete with trumpets and Christmas bells. Anxieties over the expedition fade in a magical moment of culture and time warp.

The Science Committee, it turns out, has an agenda of its own. To secure their permission for the expedition, *Calypso* must visit several areas of the province not on the Cousteau itinerary. Negotiations follow, some committee ideas are adopted, and the awaited blessing is finally given.

As Murphy and Prezelin prepare to return to *Calypso*, Premier Aule has an idea. That afternoon, he will be making his weekly radio broadcast to the islands scattered across Milne Bay. Since there are no telephones on most islands, the radio station in Alotau serves as the only link for provincial authorities with scores of villages, and for villagers the only source of news. The broadcasting fare includes an all-day educational program for the children of the province. Though there is little modern technology on most islands, there are shortwave sets in local missions, and transistor radios in many huts.

Premier Aule escorts Murphy and Prezelin to the radio station, introduces them on the air to his listeners, and invites Murphy to announce the intentions of the white ship his radio audience will soon see on the horizon.

Two tree frogs,
photographed on
Kiriwina Island in the
Trobriands, await the
night to feed in the dark
on unsuspecting insects.

For several minutes, Murphy describes the Cousteau mission to islanders who, for the most part, have never seen a television set, never seen the undersea world but for downward glimpses from their outrigger canoes or, in some cases, through wooden or plastic goggles used in hurried free dives for shellfish. Though many of the mission-educated children in the audience will have heard of France and the United States, it is unlikely many of the adults have, and perhaps no one but a scattering of foreign missionaries in the audience has ever heard of Jacques Cousteau.

"We are not coming to take anything away from your lands or your seas," Murphy tells them. "We come to observe and to learn—to learn about the beauty of your reefs and the creatures in your seas, and especially to learn from you, how you fish, how you live from and with the ocean. With our special equipment, we can show the wonders of Papua New Guinea to the rest of the world, and perhaps we can also show *you* what is hidden from you in the sea, in your own sea. We hope we can help you find ways to protect the riches of your world for generations to come by sharing what we've learned in forty years of exploring the entire planet. We come in peace, and in respect, and in friendship."

That afternoon, Albert Falco gives the order to weigh anchor, and *Calypso* sets sail eastward into Milne Bay. The tedium of preparing for an expedition gives way to the exhilaration of being off to sea, and of beginning the work of discovery once again, in a new realm, on a new campaign, with new surprises ahead.

Eumusa banana trees
are found almost
everywhere in Papua
New Guinea, though
they tend to be more
common in dry
coastal areas. Perhaps
only the sweet potato
is a more important
subsistence food crop
throughout the country.

A SEA OF JEWELS

No part of the world

exerts the same

attractive power

upon the visitor. . . .

The first love,

the first sunrise,

the first

South Sea island,

are memories apart. . . .

Robert Louis Stevenson

Cousteau divers
approach a coral head
in Deboyne Lagoon,
west of Misima
Island. For small fish
and other reef residents,
such a coral represents
a virtual undersea
city. In its crevices
countless organisms
find shelter from
predators. Many emerge
to feed only at night.

During long passages from island to island, a solitary figure often rides the bow pulpit of *Calypso*, arms folded, staring ahead for hours at a time. He sits on the windlass control box as if it were a saddle, heels on the rail cables as if they were stirrups. From this vantage point on the vessel's nose, Albert Falco studies the sky and the ocean surface for information about the conditions ahead, collecting data from the colors, temperatures, shapes, speeds, and directions of phenomena observed at sea for more than forty years.

Falco also picks up potential undersea discoveries. He notes the species of birds gathered in a feeding frenzy along the surface to starboard, and deduces the species of bait fish likely schooling beneath. He identifies far in the distance a kind of billfish, pointing at a dorsal fin visible to the rest of the crew only through binoculars.

In 1984, after three decades as Chief Diver and Expedition Leader for the Cousteaus, Albert Falco was appointed the official Captain of *Calypso*. A change in the ship's status from research vessel to private yacht, made to reduce exorbitant annual licensing fees, also made it possible to run the ship without a licensed merchant marine captain. As a result, Cousteau was finally able to put the ship under the command of the person best prepared for the job, the man called affectionately by his mates "Bebert."

With the possible exception of Simone Cousteau, who adopted the vessel as a traveling home when her husband acquired it in 1950, no one had spent as much time aboard. And no one, not even Captain Cousteau, had observed for so long and from so many perspectives the vessel's reactions to stress, its limits, its maneuverability, its speeds, its moods. What is more, as a sailor who had risen from the deck to the bridge, Bebert understood the psychological dimensions of the ship at work. He understood when a stern leader was needed, when a friend or teacher was needed.

Perhaps as important to the Cousteaus as all of these acquired abilities, Falco remains among the premier divers in the world. Though an unsuccessful operation on his sinuses impaired his underwater range several years ago, he dives nearly every day. With the native understanding and inward quiet of an Indian scout, he dons mask, fins, and snorkel shortly after anchoring the ship, then makes a wide reconnaissance around *Calypso* to determine the best sites for diving and filming. Despite his damaged sinuses, he frustrates crew members assigned the task of following him from above in a Zodiac, strict policy when someone is below. Unlike the other divers, whose bubbles boil along the surface and reveal their whereabouts, Bebert emits few bubbles. He breathes slowly underwater, while ranging along the bottom like a barracuda stalking prey. The result is that when he finally surfaces, the Zodiac and its beleaguered driver are often far away. The driver apologizes, but Bebert knows and smiles; knows that only another with such highly developed water senses could possibly track him.

When the Dive Team descends, he swims on the surface above, studying their every move, directing with a flick of his hand the position of the tender Zodiac, where two men run a generator and feed lighting cable to the team below. It is an uncommon role for a ship's captain, but an immense bonus on a ship that is carrying out uncommon work.

Thus, as *Calypso*'s diving team begins its exploration of the undersea world of Papua New Guinea, Falco is the first to enter the water. Following suggestions from Dick Murphy and local divers, he has initially steered the ship to a series of small reefs in Bentley Bay near Normanby Island, along the north side of a finger of land jutting eastward from Alotau. Descending as soon as the ship is anchored at each site, Falco finds sloping ledges and great swaths of the bottom densely covered in corals. Though fish populations vary with each dive site, he is mesmerized by the glittering colors of the schools that hover around him, apparently curious.

The team's expectations—that marine creatures here will not be as wary as those in seas widely explored by divers—seem valid: hordes of tiny basslets called jewelfish stay just beyond reach, as if accompanying him; bulb-eyed red squirrel fish watch him motionlessly, ready to dart into the caves they haunt; a school of jacks appears and surrounds the silver-suited diver, revolving about him until he starts to swim, then dashing away in a gleaming cloud.

Yet these first glimpses into the sea reveal a problem, too. Because the wet season is just ending, rivers pouring off the mainland and nearby islands have loaded the sea with silt. Visibility, while adequate for observation, is too limited to capture the sweeping richness and beauty of the reefs on film. Though Prezelin, Davis, and underwater still photographer Didier Noirot follow Falco into the water with their cameras, they are largely restricted to microphotography. In close-ups, they can cleanly record the hues of coral polyps and the tiny basslets and blennies that dwell among them.

The team soon realizes that they will have to search on their own for ideal dive sites. The advantages of diving in waters that are little explored are matched by the disadvantages: most of the vast undersea expanse off Papua New Guinea has never been seen by humans, and where it has, the

Albert Falco inspects a coral off Goodenough Island. By constructing broad leaflike colonies, coral polyps increase their surface area to enhance the collecting of sunlight. The result is an animal form closely resembling that of a plant; a similar need creates a similar structure.

Captain Falco shows
local islanders around
Calypso's bridge.

tips gained from local divers often prove unreliable. A reef that excited several scuba divers weeks earlier is now greatly changed, perhaps by the cycle of the seasons, or weather, or some unknown phenomena.

The team turns for help to Dinah and Bob Halstead, who have probably seen more of the undersea world around Papua New Guinea than anyone. The couple operates a sport-diving business that takes visitors to sites throughout the waters of eastern and northern Papua New Guinea. Near Normanby Island, *Calypso* meets up with the Halsteads and their boat *Telita*, and with their daughter Telita, an accomplished diver who has also served as a guide and translator for Murphy.

The Halsteads direct the team to a place called Doubilet Reef, named for veteran *National Geographic* magazine photographer David Doubilet. The reef represents but a tiny dot on *Calypso*'s navigational chart.

J.-M. C.: For our divers, the waters of Papua New Guinea seem a kind of liquid Eden. Ichthyologists have so far recorded more than 2,000 species of fish here. By comparison, the Caribbean supports only about 600 species. And there are undoubtedly many species in the Solomon Sea, the Coral Sea, and the Bismarck Sea that have not yet been identified. There are, as well, shellfish abundant in species and numbers; and there is a wealth of the sea's larger creatures — marine turtles, dugongs, crocodiles, dolphins, whales, and more.

Such diversity occurs because several marine zones converge here, creating an overlapping effect among species. Some marine animals in Papua New Guinea's waters have relatives in the seas of Indonesia, some in the waters of the Solomon Islands to the southeast, and some in northern Australia. During Calypso's last mission, along the Great Barrier Reef of Australia, the team encountered a similar diversity of life, yet here the reefs are as yet unaffected by waves of tourists and divers.

During the moments following our first descents in Papua New Guinea, our divers share an infectious sense of excitement as they emerge from the water. The character of these men does not allow them to exaggerate or shout effusively about some magical moment undersea. One sees it in Bebert's smile as he shakes his head and quietly says: "Superb." Prezelin, another old hand, is a master of understatement. "It was really quite nice," he will say evenly, and the meaning for those of us in the know is that he has just recorded some cinematic treasure.

man conveys his feelings differently, just as each of them has a distinc-
le in the water. Our Chief Diver Bertrand Sion is a large man with
hulking strength, as solid as a tree, and often as silent. On the deck after a dive,
Sion is taciturn as he directs the divers and oversees the cleaning and storage of
their equipment. All business until, hours later, as we sit idly in the carré (the
mess hall), he suddenly grows animated, arms waving, as he describes some
moment during the dive or teases a fellow crew member.

Chuck Davis, an American cameraman who has joined us to back up Prezelin above and below water, is another strong man, smaller than Sion but
similarly powerful. Yet in the water, he is as graceful as a marine creature,
neatly bending and knifing into the water, causing barely a ripple. On the deck,
he is the eternal optimist, certain that the unfound species can be found tomorrow, that the malfunctioning equipment can be fixed. His way of registering
enthusiasm is to describe technically what he has seen, drawing on a wide
knowledge of marine biology, and to gently insert adjectives of approval, punc-
tuated here and there with a chuckle that signifies an unspoken awe.

Among the camera team, our still photographer Didier Noirot is the least
solemn. Lighthearted and full of humor, Noirot returns from a dive to regale us
with tales of his exploits and his artistry. An experienced diver who has photographed undersea realms around the world, and has worked at jobs as varied
as electrician and farmer, he has a skilled eye and a talent for finding scenes
and creatures of beauty.

The four men whose underwater work is recorded by our cameras—
divers Antoine Rosset, Sylvain Pascaud, Thierry Dupisson, and Jean-Luc
Gourmelen—are a pleasure to watch. With previous experience as commercial
divers, for the most part, they have joined the Cousteau team to switch from
the sometimes onerous tasks associated with work like oil-rig diving, to the
more inspiring assignments of a research and filming vessel. Dupisson and
Pascaud are both tall and lanky men, with fluid motions in the sea. Rosset is a
smooth and athletic diver, who has also shown great presence of mind in times
of danger. Gourmelen, the smallest of the group, is steady and dependable, and
has proven his agility in carrying out the cumbersome task of handling the
cables for the underwater lights needed for photography.

All four, because of their youth and lack of seniority, are called upon as
deckhands as well as divers, so whatever glamour they may find as cinema subjects is tempered by the unending drudgery of sharing night watches, operating
Zodiacs and cranes and windlasses, handling lines, and carrying everything
from the chef's potato sacks to the cameraman's tripod.

The delicate shell of a
carnivorous tun snail
sits atop the creature's
head and greatly
expanded foot.

Among the most
common reef
inhabitants in the
southwest Indo-Pacific
are many species of
brilliantly colored
fusiliers. Gathered in
large schools, they
provide an abundant
source of food for
larger fish and sharks.
This individual,
photographed during
a night dive, appears
to be seeking refuge
near a sea fan. Its
nocturnal colors may
differ from those
during daylight.

Yet for all the hard work, all seem to share with my father and me the same feeling of great privilege to be leading this life, to spend day after day studying, recording, marveling at sights beyond the edges of civilization. Here, gliding among fish still unafraid of humans, descending into places perhaps no person has ever visited before, we are reminded almost hourly of the incredible fecundity and variety of life on earth.

For us, immersed in the wilderness in ways unavailable to most of humanity, the habitats and creatures we see become priceless treasures, and we constantly wonder if we are among the last to see them as civilization advances relentlessly into the remaining wild places on the planet. It is my experience that the best divers, who truly relish their time below the sea surface, are fervent ecologists. They worry deeply that this world of mysteries and surprises and amazing life may gradually disappear, eliminating a measure of personal joy from their own lives. As we enter the waters of Papua New Guinea and begin to witness its wonders, we are simultaneously enchanted by what endures here and distressed by the knowledge that it lies in the path of onrushing change.

A scorpion fish nestles into a soft coral (*Sarcophyton*) along the bottom of Deboyne Lagoon. Scorpion fish present a hazard for villagers who swim or hunt food in the shallows; their toxin-coated dorsal spines inflict extreme pain if the creature is inadvertently touched or stepped upon.

In Bob, Dinah, and Telita Halstead, the divers of *Calypso* find kindred souls. Though their business is to bring tourists into the waters of Papua New Guinea, the Halsteads follow an uncompromising environmental ethic. Spear guns are not allowed aboard their vessel, and souvenirs of coral or other bottom life cannot be removed from reefs. Ecology lessons are interspersed with cocktail parties and sunbathing. And when guests are taken ashore to mingle with villagers, a Halstead is along to ensure that the outsiders understand and respect local customs.

Their concern for the region comes naturally. Dinah is a native of Divinai, a village near Alotau. While working as a teacher, she enrolled in a diving class taught by an expatriate from England, also a schoolteacher. Bob Halstead had chosen to settle in Papua New Guinea in large part because it offered diving experiences found nowhere else. When the two were married, they set out to make a living from their love of the sea.

During the past decade, the business has grown steadily, as Australians, Japanese, and, occasionally, Americans are drawn to these pristine seas. In 1985, to meet the increasing demand for their charter tours, the Halsteads decided to build a new vessel. The MV *Telita*, completed a year later, was constructed wholly of local woods and crafted almost entirely by local villagers. At the turn of the century, a boat-building school had been established at Kwato Island in Milne Bay, producing sail and diesel work-

Overleaf: Huts of Rossel Island villagers sit at the edge of an ocean backwater rich in organic matter derived from adjacent rain-forest vegetation. Ultimately, this suspended material—washed by erosion into the sea—will be carried away by currents and will provide a source of food for nearby reef-dwelling organisms.

boats for interisland traders. Though the school continued to turn out boats for several decades, it had gradually declined. The Halsteads found the grandsons of the original shipwrights at Kwato, and with the help of Dinah's relatives and friends from Divinai, as well as a retired naval architect who had taught at the boat school fifty years earlier, they created a homegrown, home-fashioned vessel. Using hand tools and a chain saw, the team produced a 65-foot vessel outfitted with rosewood, kwil (a local hardwood), and cedar guest cabins.

For a week, *Calypso* continues on an eastward course, stopping occasionally to investigate reefs and islands in the Louisiade archipelago. On March 30th, the ship anchors at Rossel Island, where Dick Murphy has found an important film story. One goal of the expedition is to study how the people of Papua New Guinea, especially those living on the outer islands, use the ocean as a provider of sustenance and cultural goods.

Murphy has described to the team a phenomenon of Milne Bay called the Kula Ring. In the ancient rites of Kula, jewelry produced from seashells takes on an extraordinary significance.

Traveling in elaborately carved and painted Kula canoes, built solely for trading voyages, participants in the Kula Ring make an annual visit to a neighboring island. They may spend two or three weeks conducting—with consummate theatrical skills—a ceremonial exchange of treasured necklaces and armbands, jewelry which is seldom worn and serves largely as a mark of prestige. The Kula Ring follows a circular route around Milne Bay, and by custom, necklaces move clockwise from island to island, shell armbands counterclockwise. The exchanges take place between individual Kula partners, usually from neighboring islands and with few exceptions males, whose special relationship is a lifelong bond.

Neither the necklaces, called *bagi* or *veguwa*, nor the armshells, called *mwali*, can ever be considered private property. They remain a communal part of the Kula system, merely in the possession of a Kula partner for a year or two at a time. It takes about ten years for an item to complete the circuit and return to its original location. A village chief may hold dozens of Kula items, while a man of lesser standing may keep only a few.

Virtually every Kula piece has a name, and as time passes and the piece moves from island to island, it accumulates value. At all times, there are a few necklaces or armshells that have taken on legendary status and are passionately coveted by the traders. Most Kula traders know the location of these treasured pieces at all times. To keep a piece of sacred jewelry too long is to risk grave danger, since angered Kula partners can summon a measure of justice from local sorcerers.

The fascination for Kula among anthropologists comes not from the nature of the jewelry, which can be lovely, but from the social instrument of the system. Some believe this elaborate exchange of generally "useless" goods acts like an ever-renewing contract, a kind of invisible treaty, between small societies that might otherwise be hostile. The Kula Ring, they believe, prevents war by ensuring peaceful contacts and personal alliances from island to island, and by bestowing on the possessors of renowned Kula pieces a fame that, in other societies, might be gained through violent conquests.

Of the two kinds of jewelry exchanged, the necklaces are deemed more important, and it is at Rossel Island, at the western end of the Louisiade archipelago, and at the southern extreme of the Kula Ring, where the prized seashells are found that make up nearly all of the treasured *bagi*.

Fishermen near Goodenough Island in Milne Bay drop rocks from their outrigger canoes to frighten the reef fish below into crevices, then free dive to spear the cornered creatures.

A Rossel Island goggle diver returns to the surface with a rock scallop *(Chama imbricata)*. Valued for the red coloration that lines the lips of the bivalve's shells, the scallops are turned into jewelry that is the foundation of the celebrated Kula Ring of Milne Bay.

Leaving *Calypso* in Zodiacs, the film and dive teams follow several young Rossel villagers in outrigger canoes. Stopping over several submerged rocks just off the rugged coastline, the young men climb from the canoes and free dive to a depth of about 15 feet, wearing goggles and carrying axes or hammers. As the Cousteau divers hover alongside, the villagers search about for a species of rock scallop known to science as *Chama imbricata,* which is prized for a red lip along the edges of its shells. Dashing about the bottom, the divers pry the mollusks from rocks, shooting to the surface with a handful, catching a lungful of air, and descending again.

After about an hour of such diving, the young men paddle back to the village, where their catch is cooked and passed about as lunch. A young diver offers a serving to Rosset and Pascaud, who nibble on the meat and pronounce it thoroughly acceptable. After the meal, an assembly line is organized and the making of necklaces begins. At the first stop, the shells are broken into pieces with hammers. The smaller pieces are carried to a second stop, where they are further reduced in size by more hammers.

Next, salmon-red pieces of the shells are separated and further hammered into dime-sized fragments. These small red pieces are polished smooth and clean and ground on a stone using sand and water into even-sized, wafer-like discs. They are then handed to hole-makers, who use hand-operated pump drills to ream out a tiny opening in the center of each piece. When all the red discs have holes, they are strung on a twine made of pandanus root and the entire necklace, composed of 150 to 200 shell discs, is ground lengthwise so that each piece is precisely the same diameter. At each end of the necklace, following tradition, small white discs and black banana pods are added.

To an experienced Kula man, the necklaces can be appraised according to the thinness of the discs (the thinner the more valuable) and the shade and uniformity of the colors (a pale hue is more desirable than a dark hue, a rare yellow color is the most highly valued, and consistency in color is highly prized). To turn a common *bagi* into an important Kula piece, the string of discs is extended to a length of 6 to 15 feet, and adorned with a large shell pendant and fringing shell fragments.

Ironically, though most *bagi* are produced at Rossel Island—said to be the only source of the desirable rock-scallop shells—the people of the

Chama shells collected by divers on Rossel Island are first broken up with hammers. The red parts of the shells are passed to other villagers who further reduce the fragments.

Rossel Island women grind the pieces into flat disks, still rough around the edges but approximately the same size.

When the shell fragments are flat, women use hand drills to pierce the centers.

island are not participants in the Kula exchange system. Their necklaces have been bartered to other islanders for centuries in exchange for essential goods lacking on Rossel, such as clay pots, conch-shell pendants, and a species of green parrot whose plumes are worn by the wives of the island's "big men." Yet their finest creations have a near-mythical importance on other islands.

Some measure of the regard for *bagi* is provided by a story from a hundred years ago. In 1888, gold was discovered on Sudest Island, to the southwest of Rossel. Foreign miners found that they could entice the people of Sudest to help them pan for gold if they offered, not a share of the gold, but a payment in *bagis*. The shiny metal seemed insignificant compared to the revered shell necklaces.

As they prepare to leave Rossel, now fascinated by the Kula phenomenon, Rosset and Pascaud ask if they might purchase the necklace they have watched being made. No problem. The asking price is 50 kina, roughly $50. The two divers solicit the money from the keepers of *Calypso*'s cash, Falco and Simone, and the vessel leaves Rossel with a *bagi* of its own, which is carefully stowed in the glass display case in the *carré*, alongside Greek artifacts brought up during archaeological dives in the Mediterranean.

In the final step, the pieces of a necklace are ground smooth and strung together with pandanus fiber. An entire village day is spent collecting enough *Chama* shells and refining the fragments to make a single necklace. Eventually, an elaborate array of pendants of other shells and seeds are added to the necklace, turning it into a precious trading item known in the Kula Ring as a *bagi* or *soulava*.

From Rossel, the ship sails back to Alotau to board provisions sent from Moresby by Karen Brazeau, then on to Goodenough Island, where the vessel drops anchor at 3:00 A.M. At sunrise, as the crew emerges from their quarters, they confront a dramatic sight. The island is majestic, a series of green peaks thrusting up from the sea. Taking the ratio of height to width at the base, Goodenough is one of the most mountainous islands in the world.

Moreover, the ship is surrounded by some forty outrigger canoes, some carrying entire families of villagers, some with a lone teenager, some with two or three young children. All appear to be waiting patiently for the ship to awaken.

When the first crew members are sighted, three villagers scramble onto *Calypso*'s deck, asking to meet the captain. Among the boarding party is a tiny man, no taller than a child of ten, who is introduced as the local chief. The visitors are escorted to the bridge, where Falco is working on the logbook.

An impromptu tour is organized, and the curious village elders are shown the radar, the sonar, the satellite navigation system. The visitors respond politely but show little interest until someone hands the chief a pair of binoculars. Falco takes them in hand, shows how they are used, and focuses them on the chief's village. When the glasses are raised to his eyes, the old man's face freezes in a look of astonishment. It is clear to Falco that the sophisticated equipment packed around the bridge and radio room mean little to the visitors, but the binoculars, and the magical vision they afford of a familiar scene, are a thing of surpassing wonder.

By midafternoon, after the initial period of shyness has faded, more than fifty young villagers have climbed aboard *Calypso*. As the team goes about routine tasks, fueling the outboard engines, washing the decks, filling the air tanks, the young visitors watch in fascination and amusement. The grand event comes when Prezelin and the Dive Team suit up in their silver skins and dive from the rear deck to film local fishermen at work. Gathered in small groups along the rail, the visitors crane their necks, peek around corners, and lean over the side. Without their knowledge, radio officer Michel Verdier stands on the helicopter platform above recording their every move with the ship's video camera, which was purchased to compile a visual supplement to the official logbook, but more often serves as a kind of home-movie camera for the crew, offering instant replays for laughs and a useful record of work.

Late in the afternoon, the chief invites the team to visit his village, a collection of about a dozen palm-thatched huts on stilts. As dusk falls, inspired perhaps by the festive mood and friendliness of the villagers, Michel Verdier has an idea. He takes a Zodiac back to *Calypso*, loads it with an electric generator, a television monitor, appropriate cables, and the ship's video camera and player. In the center of the village, he sets the equipment up, and plays not only the cassette he has recorded earlier in the day, but cassettes taped at Rossel and other islands.

At first baffled by the odd paraphernalia, the villagers are startled by what they see when Verdier turns the monitor on. After a few moments of stunned silence, they burst out laughing as their own images appear on the screen. The entire village is summoned, and those who cannot see because of the crowd packed about the television set climb into trees for a better view. The giggles and screams of laughter continue until the visiting magicians pack up their strange boxes and return to the ship for dinner.

With reactions that range from bemusement to astonishment, Goodenough islanders watch a videotape of themselves and their village made by *Calypso*'s team. The Cousteau crew set up a monitor and portable electric generator to give villagers their first glimpse of television.

At 8:00 A.M. the next morning, the ship leaves for Fergusson Island, like Goodenough a mountainous, jungled island formed by the peaks of submerged volcanoes. At noon, as the ship approaches the southern coastline of Fergusson, Braunbeck and Prezelin lift off in the helicopter. As they will nearly every day during the coming two months, the pilot and film director make an inspection flight around the next destination, then land to meet local villagers and brief them on the arriving ship.

Beyond the airstrip, they see an open area where the verdant covering seems scorched away. The ground is pink and white, perforated by water-filled craters, some clear blue, some ocher, some white. Steam geysers rise from a few holes, mud bubbles from others. Fergusson Island, as Dick Murphy has reported, offers a dramatic illustration of the geology that is central to understanding the natural world of Papua New Guinea.

Part of the highly mobile zone of the earth's crust surrounding the Pacific Ocean, the country sits atop the collision point of several tectonic plates. Continuous folding and faulting activities, and volcanic eruptions, have shaped the mainland and islands and determined their resource bases. The result has been, across the eons, a series of uplifts of material from deep within the earth. Occasional volcanic activity has acted like a vast fertilizing system, enriching the soils, fostering dense vegetation, and ultimately, supplying life-supporting nutrients to the sea as well.

After lunch, a team is assembled to go ashore and visit the hot springs. Prezelin, Davis, sound engineer Yves Zlotnicka, assistant cameraman Raymond Amaddio, and divers Rosset and Pacaud, are accompanied by Verdier with his video camera, and the ship's medical officer, Dr. François Raineix. Worried that the adventurous crew might meet with an accident, Raineix carries a large bag of medical supplies and burn creams.

Steam geysers and boiling mud holes on Fergusson Island attest to the fiery subterranean world below most of Papua New Guinea.

Women of Fergusson Island routinely take advantage of the boiling hot springs near their village to cook food and wash laundry, a free service provided by the planetary furnace hidden miles below. Cousteau team members, who found the ground unbearably hot through heavy boots, marveled at the endurance of islanders walking the area barefoot.

As they walk the mile between the shore and the hot springs, a handful of young people appear and tag along. By the time the entourage has arrived at what resembles an empty moonscape, the onlookers have grown to a crowd of more than a hundred. Having reluctantly followed the doctor's advice to wear heavy shoes, the team is surprised now to see that the women working around the edges of the boiling natural cauldrons are barefoot. Soon, however, the men realize that the ground is frying hot. They can feel the heat rising through the thick soles of their shoes. That the natives of Fergusson can walk upon such a blistering ground without shoes fills the Cousteau team with amazement.

During the second day at Fergusson, while the divers are below exploring its marine settings, Falco receives word that the entire crew has been invited to a welcoming party in their honor at a village on Fergusson. The team members have read in their research notebooks about the festive dances commonly called singsings held in most Papua New Guinea villages. Depending on the location of the village and its exposure to tourists, singsings can range from traditional ceremonies little changed for centuries to shows performed for a price.

On Fergusson, which is on a shipping route and receives occasional visits from *Telita* and other small tour boats, there has been significant outside influence. Most of the villagers wear western clothes, perhaps encouraged by the local Christian mission, which has also spread the English language among most of the children. The singsing here seems a bizarre blend of ancient ways and the villagers' fascination with what they have seen of the modern world.

As the Cousteau team makes its way from the beach to the singsing site—where mats, a bench, and a table have been set up among knolls behind the village—a group of native men adorned in feathers and shells and with gaudily painted faces, suddenly rush the team. With spears raised threateningly, they dance about the visitors to the sound of drums, occasionally taunting an individual crewman, pumping their spears as if they are about to pierce him.

Though reasonably confident that the hostile greeting is merely part of the show, a few crew members are left temporarily unsettled. Then, with the same suddenness in which the "welcoming" committee has appeared on the path to the village, the dancers now abruptly turn and walk away. As the men disappear, a knot of women appears, some wearing branches around their waists from which hang green palm nuts the size and color of limes. The Cousteau crew has seen betel nuts on Rossel and learned that these common seeds are chewed for their mildly narcotic effects, but until now they have not realized how pervasive the habit of chewing betel nuts is in the cultures of Papua New Guinea. It is, they are told, the country's equivalent of drinking beer.

As a result of the practice, nearly everyone in the village has discolored teeth, ranging from red to black. Most of the village men carry some kind of knit bag over their shoulders in which they keep the paraphernalia of the betel nut chewer: a supply of the green nuts; a container (often a decorated gourd, but sometimes an empty plastic ketchup bottle or peanut butter jar) filled with the lime powder that acts as a catalyst to heighten the effect of the narcotic; several sprigs of a variety of pepper plant, which, when chewed with the nut-lime mixture, seems to soften the acrid taste; and a utensil used to spoon the lime from its container, sometimes a carved wooden blade, sometimes a cassowary bone.

Proudly displaying their handcrafted baskets, a family assembles before a Cousteau camera in a village near Mount Hagen.

The team is led to wooden benches and palm mats, and when everyone is seated, the dancing begins. As the evening winds on, village women invite the team to partake of the refreshments laid out on a table behind them: rice, yams, several kinds of vegetable stews, fruit juice, and coconuts. In the spirit of hospitality, they also offer betel nuts to anyone willing to try them. The only taker this night, though many will experiment before the expedition is over, is Teriihaunui Loyat, a deckhand and diver who had joined the crew some months earlier during the team's Tahiti expedition. Since no one aboard can pronounce the young Tahitian's name, they have come to call him "Maupiti," after the island of his birth. With a buoyant spirit, a quick sense of humor, and a native sense of the sea, he has quickly endeared himself to the rest of the crew.

While Prezelin and Davis film the singsing, Zlotnicka adds a commentary as he records the ambient sounds and music, inquiring of nearby villagers the theme of each dance. The initial dances seem to represent village myths, spiritual symbols, and aspects of daily life. The dancers are crows at one point, then chickens, then babies in their mothers' arms. They imitate the paddling of canoes, the swimming of a river, the gathering of yams. An hour passes, then another.

Finally, a villager tells Zlotnicka that the dancers are about to perform the last two dances of the evening. The next one, he is told, is the dance of a lady using a typewriter.

"They will dance like a typewriter?" he asks in astonishment.

"Yes."

"And the last dance. What will they imitate in that dance?"

"A forklift driver," he is told.

J.-M. C.: Watching this strange amalgam of spiritualism and materialism, we wonder if the dances are not the latest manifestation of an historical phenomenon called "cargo cults." In the middle of the nineteenth century, when foreigners began to arrive in New Guinea in significant numbers, islanders were shocked by the miraculous goods the strangers unloaded from the cargo holds of their ships. To a people who still prized obsidian for their tools and weapons, the appearance of steel axes, rifles, and the like seemed an event of supernatural doing. Since their own beliefs held that everything is supplied from the spirit world, they reasoned that by following powerful new rituals they might call up some of these new products for themselves.

Knowing that their established rites would not work, they incorporated the behavior of the visitors into their society, anticipating that like behavior would produce like results. On some islands, docks were built so that ships might arrive from the spirit world bearing modern equipment. Observing that the foreigners had a kind of fetish for bureaucracy, villagers constructed thatched hut "offices," where they passed pieces of paper back and forth to one another.

With the arrival of airplanes, rough airstrips were hewn from the forest to accommodate the expected arrival of planes piloted from the spirit world by their dead ancestors. When telephones arrived in some parts of Papua New Guinea, mock telephones made of tin cans appeared in the "offices" of cargo cultists.

Of course, the rituals proved worthless. Nothing ever arrived, and gradually cargo cultists lost their enthusiasm. The phenomenon would nearly die out, only to be revived every few decades when a new wave of foreigners appeared.

Though amused by such tales, we have not found the people of Papua New Guinea's islands as innocent or naive as these stories would suggest. At Rossel, Goodenough, and Fergusson our impressions have been of a people who, while marveling at some of our equipment, do not seem to covet greatly our material goods. They have adopted factory-made items of clothing for the most part, and they now use steel axes instead of traditional stone tools. They have learned to trade their carvings, baskets, and clay pots for cash, where once they used shells as currency.

Yet so far we have not seen people wearing watches, and while one occasionally hears recorded music drifting from a hut, the cassettes being played are not the latest rock-and-roll albums but traditional island music. Our impressions are that islanders here, while interested in new gadgets, are not driven to have them, are not yet caught up in the fast pace of the faraway industrial world. They are, or so it seems, a people still largely content with the abundant products of nature. We have seen a few containers of store-bought juices, but the most common remedy for thirst remains a coconut. Villagers hack a clean opening in the top with a machete, sip the cool juice, then break up the shell and share the white meat inside. Most of our crew, in fact, have come to relish this refreshment.

For some of us, these first days of contact have produced a kind of reverse cultural yearning. Though the heat can be oppressive, we admire the comfortable rhythms of life here, the quick smiles about us, the genial hospitality extended to strangers.

We are amazed by the villagers' encyclopedic knowledge of the surrounding environment. Every item necessary to survival, perhaps even to happiness, can be drawn from land, forest, or sea. Perhaps it takes village men longer to cross an ocean strait in an outrigger canoe propelled by a pandanus sail than it takes us in our motor vessel. But the speed of such a trip may be largely irrelevant in a world ungoverned by clocks, unstressed by deadlines other than those imposed by nature—by the rhythms of daylight and dark, by the directions of the wind, by the pulse of the seasons.

In meetings aboard Calypso, *it is decided that we will spend the coming weeks further investigating the Kula Ring to witness the various steps of this curious, peace-ensuring tradition. We will also seek to learn how islanders here capture and utilize the bountiful foods of the sea. And we will push farther from the Papua New Guinea mainland, to search for peoples even more removed from the modern world than the islanders we have so far encountered.*

On the morning of April 10th, Bebert steers Calypso *into the open waters east of Fergusson Island. When the ship is well under way, he turns the wheel over to Sion and walks to the bow. There, seated comfortably on the windlass control box, arms folded, he fastens his eyes and mind on the waters ahead. Watching, I am struck by the similarity between Albert Falco and the village chiefs we have met. Like them, he acts from years of experience with, and a deep intuitive understanding of, the world of nature. Like them, he directs his people with a soft voice and leads with a quiet authority. Like them, he appreciates the fate of the human being, to be at once the most potent creature on earth and a fragile organism at the mercy of the great sea and sky about him.*

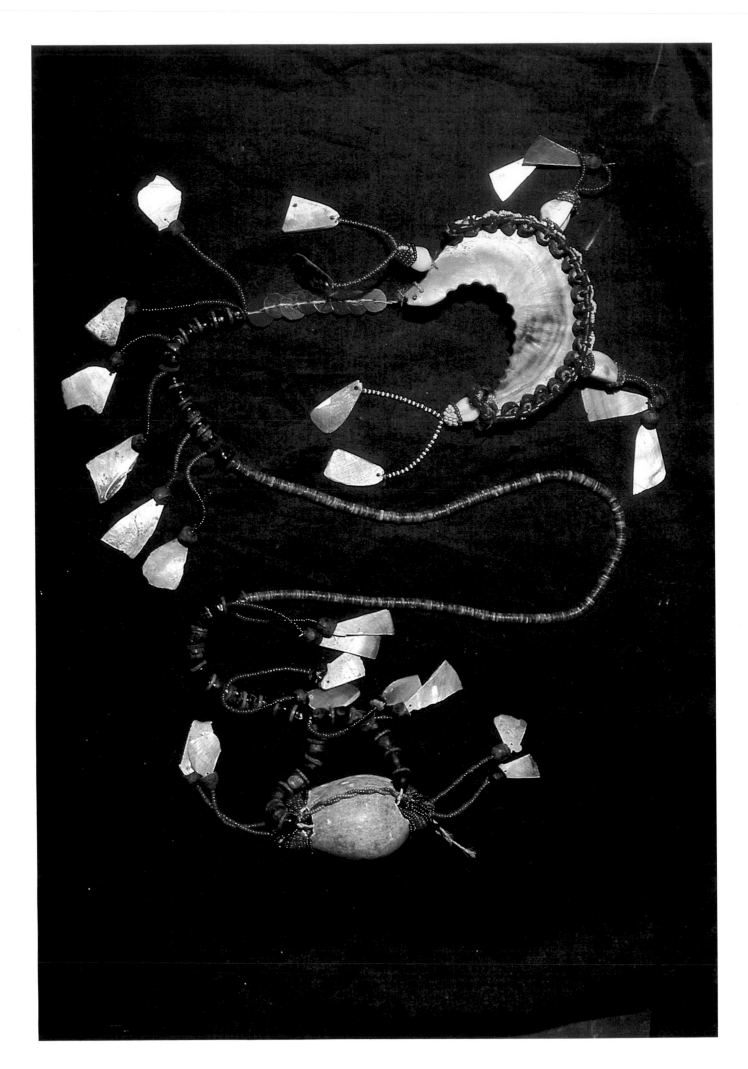

A NECKLACE NAMED CALYPSO

It will last

forever,

until the end

of the world.

Maik Elliot,

Kula partner

A traditional *bagi* necklace is adorned with the accessory items that will make it valuable on the Kula Ring. To the string of *Chama* shell disks in the center have been added black banana seeds and shell pendants. Cowrie and mother-of-pearl *(kina)* shells are attached to each end. Recently, glass and plastic beads have been integrated into the necklaces.

As *Calypso* sails eastward at full speed into the open waters at the center of Milne Bay Province, a day and night pass without the sighting of an island or even another vessel at sea. While the watch crews rotate on four-hour shifts—following the course penciled onto the navigational chart by Falco, making hourly visits to the smokestack through the night to check for stack fires, entering locations and times in the logbook—the atmosphere of life aboard changes. For many, the hours of a passage serve as the seagoing equivalent of a weekend, though usually compressed into a matter of hours.

The Film Team, which scrambles to capture film images above and below the water while the ship is at anchor, often retires to their bunks to catch up on sleep while the ship is en route. But to sleep, they must learn to ignore the squeaks and groans of the old wooden ship and to slumber even as their bodies are rolling and pitching with the motions of the ship.

Early on the morning of April 11th, *Calypso* approaches a knob of volcanic rock that sits alone in an empty expanse of water. Round, with sheer walls carved away at the base by waves and a topping of vegetation and palm trees, it looks to the crew like a great birthday cake on a display stand. The ship's arrival sends hundreds of birds rising into the air from the top of the rocky cake, and scores of black-and-white butterflies, some of which wander to *Calypso*'s deck and alight on the crew's shoulders.

Since the Halsteads have suggested this as an interesting dive site, Falco orders the crew to drop anchor and to find a mooring spot to ensure that the vessel is secured. The divers and camera crew, meanwhile, motor in Zodiacs to the far side of the rock and enter the water in search of pelagic fish (normally hard to find in open water), which, they reason, might be drawn to this lonely outpost in the trackless sea seeking local fish and crustaceans dwelling along its submerged base. For two hours they film schools of tuna and jacks, but the water is too murky for good shots and they eventually return frustrated.

Four hours later, *Calypso* arrives at Iwa Island, another rock cake rising from the sea, this one perhaps three miles across. Through binoculars, the men on the bridge count seven Kula canoes on the beach. Prezelin and Braunbeck visit the island in the helicopter, *Felix,* returning to announce that not only is a Kula exchange in progress but the men of Iwa catch fish in a bizarre fashion earlier described by Dick Murphy. They snag them with spider-webs.

To reach the two villages on the island, which sit on a plateau, the team must make a thirty-minute climb up steps cut into a rocky wall. Prezelin decides to send the heavy film equipment, as well as Davis and Zlotnicka, on ahead by helicopter. The rest of the team will climb the steep slope.

Hours later, the group sets out to scale the vertical path to the top of the island. Midway, drenched in perspiration and out of breath, one team member observes that a particularly rotund member of the crew fortunately has stayed aboard because had he come, he would be struggling. Raymond Amaddio, whose dry wit invariably raises team spirits, calls out from the rear of the procession: "Yes. It would have taken him two trips."

The mood of buoyancy is soon stilled. As the men enter the first of two villages, they pass a sad scene. An infant born prematurely has died only hours before. In the hut of its parents, a dozen people are wailing in profound despair. The rest of the village is quiet. Children from throughout the island, who have crowded about the crew upon arrival, lead them past the mourners and onto the next village, where the "big man" of Iwa—

Calypso anchors along a limestone cliff bordering tiny Iwa Island in Milne Bay. Diving from the ship, the Cousteau team found a sheer vertical undersea wall festooned with brilliantly colored corals and sea fans.

Dancers on Iwa Island celebrate the annual yam harvest with an elaborate *singsing*. Cockatoo feathers serve as headdresses, chains of betel nuts are strung as necklaces. *Singsing* is a generic Pidgin English word used throughout the country for village dances, which may celebrate a variety of events, from seasonal feasts to initiation rites to marriages.

A teenage Iwa Island *singsing* dancer wears the costume she will don once a year for the sacred yam dances. Only a few dozen villagers, trained from an early age, perform *singsing* dances. The youngster illustrates not only the fine features of Melanesians but the source of the word Papua—a holdover from early Dutch explorers who dubbed New Guinea the land of the "Fuzzy Hairs" (*Papuas* in Dutch).

Chief Wadilei—has organized a singsing in honor of *Calypso*'s visit. Weeks earlier, Dick Murphy made a stop at Iwa in *Papagallo* to explain the purpose of the expedition. Through the schoolmaster's radio, the children say, they also heard a foreign man talking about a white ship. Murphy's radio broadcast from Alotau, the men note, has reached at least one island along the expedition route.

The welcoming singsing this first evening on Iwa greatly resembles the dancing on Fergusson Island, except that the themes are traditional. (The people of Iwa have not been exposed to typewriters or forklifts.) Prezelin learns that the ship's arrival could not have been more fortuitous. The owners of the canoes sighted earlier on the beach are men from the island of Kitava, some twenty miles to the northwest. They are here for a Kula exchange with their Iwa partners. Moreover, the next night will be given over, not only to Kula rites, but to a great singsing and yam festival which occurs on Iwa only once every five or six years.

The next morning—after the ritual *Calypso* breakfast of toast, marmalade, peanut butter, and coffee—Davis, Pascaud, and Noirot rendezvous with two local fishermen. The Cousteau team is eager to watch and to film the practice of fishing with spiderwebs. They are led behind a village into dense jungle still moist with dew. While the fishermen gather the webs, Davis and Noirot follow with their cameras.

Following a practice centuries old, fishermen on Iwa Island gather spiderwebs from the forest to fabricate an unusual natural snare to capture marine fish called needlefish or gars.

When a sufficient collection of webs has been accumulated, the men search from the island's high cliffs for a spot likely to be abundant in needlefish.

A fisherman releases a line to which spider-webs have been attached. The kite causes the lure to dance across the surface of the water, and when the curious needlefish attack the webs, their teeth and jaws become inextricably entangled.

When they have accumulated a supply of webs, the fishermen descend to the beach. Under their arms they carry small kites made from leaves, reinforced by twigs. They hang the spider webs from a long kite tail made of twine, then paddle offshore, sailing against the wind so that it lofts the kite above the water. The tail and spiderwebs skip across the surface, acting as a lively lure. Attracted by the sight or sound of the dancing lures, needlefish (also called gars) rise to the surface and attack. When their jaws are entangled in the spiderwebs, the fishermen draw the kite in.

J.-M. C.: Our team has noticed a curious thing. Understandably, they are met at each island by a throng of children, for whom the sudden appearance of an unusual ship bearing men who carry odd things down into the sea must be a remarkable event. Yet the surprise is that, almost invariably, when they greet the team the first words from their mouths are: "We are Christians." We can only surmise that they associate us with the other outsiders whose looks are similar to ours—missionaries—and they seek to welcome us immediately with words of cultural fellowship.

The impact of Christian missions has been powerful throughout Papua New Guinea. Though the ancient tribal beliefs handed down through generations are still important—dictating most of the values and rituals—nearly every primal religion has been affected by Christianity. Catholics, Lutherans, Methodists, Anglicans, Seventh-Day Adventists, Evangelicals, and London Missionary Society field workers had all arrived by the end of the last century, most establishing missions on the islands of the Solomon and Bismarck seas.

The surge in missionary activity, however, came on the heels of World War II, when scores of churches began building missions in every province. By the 1950s, the Salvation Army, Jehovah's Witnesses, and the Baha'i faith had arrived. Today, nearly half of the population is claimed by the Roman Catholic Church and two Lutheran churches.

As in most areas of the world, missionaries have accomplished changes both laudable and regrettable. The chief of Goodenough Island told Rosset and Pascaud that missionaries had brought peace to the island, eliminating internal and intertribal violence. In many cases we have seen that missions and churches have contributed to the advancement of education and medical services throughout the country.

Yet there have been undesirable results as well. A vast treasury of native art has been destroyed over the years by missionaries who considered it blasphemous. And we wonder about the effects of the Christian teachings that inculcate a sense of sin and guilt in a people who have traditionally drawn their ethics from the natural environment around them. Our concern is not so much that something new is being learned but that something ancient, inspiring an intimacy and a harmony with nature, is being lost.

On Iwa, the effects of outside civilization seem largely confined to a mission school, which is run by a native Papua New Guinean. The population is neatly divided by age. Those above about twenty do not read, nor do they speak English. Nearly everyone below twenty years of age speaks at least rudimentary

Dependent upon the sea for sustenance and for travel, young Iwa Islanders learn early the skills of seafaring and fishing. Fashioning toy outriggers with leaf sails, boys mimic the great Kula canoes of their elders, racing them for hours at a time in the shallows.

Using models of traditional huts, youngsters in a Trobriand cultural heritage class learn how to thatch a roof with palm leaves.

English. It is a testament to the children's eagerness to learn that they ask of us not candy or shiny gadgets but pens, pencils, and notepads with which to write their lessons. Dick Murphy, inspired by this, has arranged for a shipment of school materials to be sent here by The Cousteau Society.

In general, whatever their contacts with the faraway world, children here seem full of friendliness and joy. Boys and girls alike wear red hibiscus blooms in their hair. They surround us in fervent excitement, yet remain polite and shy, at the same time ardently trying to get close enough to offer each of us a handshake.

Returning to the ship from the villages of Iwa, the Cousteau team is in a breezy mood, charmed by the islanders. Sion has purchased a carved toy for his niece in France, an ebony bird that bobs as it slides down pandanus twine strung on a bow. The team has returned with a carved pig for Simone, who was amused by one seen at a previous island.

The next afternoon, leaving only the watch crew aboard, the ship's crew attends en masse the grand singsing on Iwa Island. It is the most elaborate they have yet seen. The dancers are decorated in stark black and white. Half of a body may be painted black, half white, in vegetable dyes. Elegant facial designs are also black and white. Aromatic flowers and grasses are tucked into armbands. Glistening coconut oil coats the skin. White cockatoo feathers and black cassowary plumes are stuck in their hair. The effect is visually arresting. While most of the dancers are men, a dozen or so bare-breasted young women file along at the end of the procession.

As the dancers enter the central square of the village, the team watches a scene that cuts across the gulf between this culture and their own. As the young girls join the dance, mothers rush alongside adjusting their skirts and feathers, shouting directions. Though the Cousteau team cannot understand the language, the admonitions seem to be about standing up straight and paying attention. "Mothers," someone remarks, "are the same everywhere."

Around the square, yams have been piled up in roped pens that rise eight feet from the ground. Branches laden with betel nuts sit atop the pens, bananas and sugarcane are heaped around the bottom. Yams hold a significance that reverberates throughout the island cultures. The yam is, after all, the most important staple food, storable for long periods of time and grown to the size of a large Idaho potato or a small log, depending on

To preserve their traditional ways in the face of imported products and practices, Trobriand villages devote one school day each week to cultural heritage. Students wear traditional dress and learn the beliefs and crafts of the ancients. Here, a young boy uses a carving adz.

the variety. Yet they are also a kind of cultural currency fraught with value and symbolic meaning. A couple eat yams together to announce their marriage. A man's accumulation of yams is a measure of his wealth. His ability to grow a fine yam garden is one of the traits that defines his character.

When the singsing dancing winds down after several hours, a cluster of elders headed by Chief Wadilei moves from one yam pen to another. Wadilei calls out the names of villages and families at each pen, thus assigning the foodstuffs. The yams, fruits, and betel nuts gradually fan out among the crowd, most of whom sit cross-legged on the ground working intently on their betel nuts and lime.

Finally, as Prezelin and Davis film, two elders begin a ritual of Kula exchange. Maik Elliot, a young Iwa man who speaks English, stands alongside the ship's crew translating the proceedings. One Kula partner is from Kitava and has been sleeping on the local beach for two weeks. The other man is from this village on Iwa. They may have been partners for several decades, annually passing Kula pieces only to one another. While the Iwa man sits quietly before his hut, eyes locked in a stare that never wavers, the Kitava man arrives carrying a long *bagi*, which jangles like a cluster of rattles as he walks.

Seeing the event begin, and drawn also by the Cousteau camera team, scores of villagers crowd around. The Kitava man, when he is only ten feet from his motionless partner, erupts in a series of shouts and insults. Standing in a circle around the two men, children begin to laugh uproariously. What would seem to the Cousteau team a tense encounter turns out to be a kind of vaudeville performance.

The Kitava man, who has held the valuable necklace for a year or so, launches into a diatribe about how undeserving his partner is of this magnificent necklace. He is not worthy enough to be on the same island

In the Kiriwina Island village of Okaiboma, noted for its production of hardwood bowls shaped as marine creatures, a carver named Amos uses pig snout to polish a fish bowl. Trobriand carvers were once noted for their ebony artifacts, but overexploitation of the wood for carvings led to the depletion of ebony on the island. Today, some carvers simply stain their works with black shoe polish to give the appearance of ebony.

with this glorious necklace. He has done nothing in all of his life to warrant even a brief glimpse at this most important and exquisite necklace, which is undoubtedly the finest necklace in the world. The crowd cackles.

Now the tone of the speech changes slightly. Even though his partner does not have the kind of qualities desired in a man who would hold this necklace . . . even though his partner has treated *him* maliciously over the years . . . even though his partner has refused to pass along valuable Kula items to *him* . . . he, Naluwa of Kitava, is a man of the most extraordinary generosity, and he will illustrate his superior qualities by passing this matchless necklace on to his inferior partner.

Suddenly, the Kitava man tosses his *bagi* across the shoulder of his Iwa partner, who still has not moved his eyes or changed his rigid expression. To show his reciprocal disdain, the Iwa man remains frozen in his seat as the necklace slips off his shoulder onto the ground. It is promptly retrieved, however, by a family member of the Iwa partner and carried into the hut behind him. After another outburst from the Kitava man, and more swells of laughter, the presenter turns on his heels quickly and disappears. The *bagi*, it seems, has been accepted.

Antoine Rosset turns to Maik Elliot and asks him if, as schools and missions change their society, the Kula Ring will someday disappear? The young man does not think so. He himself is already a Kula partner at the age of nineteen. "It will last forever," he says, "until the end of the world."

About dawn on the morning of April 14th, *Calypso* arrives along the northern shore of Kiriwina, largest of the Trobriand Islands. The ship, however, can stay here no longer than a day before sailing back to its current supply port of Alotau. Using a ton of fuel each day at anchor, and three to four tons underway, the vessel must refuel about every two weeks. In the past, there was also a need to refill water tanks, but desalination units now turn seawater into an unlimited supply of fresh water. Chef Patrick Bernard is running low on fresh foods, though. Meat can be frozen in a locker below deck, but the ship must take fresh fruits and vegetables aboard about every two weeks.

Since *Calypso*'s round-trip sail to Alotau will take as long as five days, a Land Team is organized to remain on Kiriwina: Prezelin, Zlotnicka, Davis, Amaddio, Rosset, Pascaud, Noirot, and Mose Richards. By afternoon, after Prezelin and Braunbeck have shuttled about by helicopter to make lodging and travel arrangements, the Land Team departs the ship to remain on the island for a week.

They are conveyed across the island by minivan, over the lone coral road that runs north and south, to Kiriwina Lodge in the town of Losuia. The manager, a blond-haired Australian expatriate named Bill Rudd, greets the crew and gets them settled into rooms. Since it is now late in the afternoon, there is little to do but visit the crocodile cage in the front yard, order up some cold beer, and relax.

Rudd eventually sits down with the team and answers their questions about the island. Like many expatriates in Papua New Guinea—the universal term here is "expats"—he appears to have left his native country in search of untapped entrepreneurial horizons and a pace of life more fit to his temperament. He married an island woman, had a bevy of children, started a doomed business in Moresby, and came to the Trobriands on a lark to turn a friend's guest house into a small hotel. That was nearly twenty years ago. Except for a few missionaries, he is the only expat in

permanent residence here, and he relishes the life and culture. He has not worn more than T-shirt, shorts, and thong sandals for months, and he has, over the years, become a member in good standing of the Kula Ring, the only white member to his knowledge.

He leads the team to his house, adjoining the lodge, and displays his treasures: several *bagi* necklaces, some *mwali* armbands, and shelves stocked with the raw materials to fabricate the jewelry. Rudd, it turns out, has become a maker of Kula items, which he christens with the names of his children and friends. He agrees to take the Cousteau team to a local village where a Kula boat has just returned from Kitava Island.

Rudd introduces a young Trobriander named Jerome Koubuli, and suggests that the team employ him as a guide. Jerome, they soon learn, has a fascinating story to tell. He recently graduated from the University of Papua New Guinea with a degree in economics. But when he contemplated a career in Port Moresby, he found the prospect bleak. By comparison, life on Kiriwina offered him, he says, all of the things ambitious young people strive to earn money to purchase.

Jerome, it turns out, is the nephew of the most important chief on Kiriwina—the "Paramount Chief." Because the society is matrilineal and power is passed on to a chief's sister's son, he is next in line to inherit the title. As such, he will have several wives (the last Paramount Chief had eleven), a never-ending supply of food and betel nuts, and the utter devotion of every Kiriwina native, which Rudd and Jerome estimate at about 19,000 people living in sixty villages. In this male-dominant society, with his status as an island prince, he also has abundant sexual opportunities among young single island girls—opportunities it seems he has not ignored.

"Why should I work?" he asks. "To buy a Mercedes? A fine automobile is not practical here and I don't need it to attract a pretty face. To accumulate wealth? What would I do with it? Buy a vacation to a beautiful tropical island like the one I already live on?"

The Cousteau team nods, thinking.

The first order of business on the following day is to meet with the Paramount Chief and secure his blessings for the week of filming on Kiriwina. Jerome has explained the importance of this meeting by recounting the story of a Japanese film team that arrived on the island a few years ago to shoot a documentary. They saw no reason to talk to the Paramount Chief because they had in their possession letters of authorization from the central and district governments.

When the Chief learned of their intentions, he summoned them to his village and asked for an explanation. They produced the papers and detailed all of the authorities who had given them permission. The Paramount Chief told them to leave the island immediately, which they did, without taking away a frame of film.

Jerome accompanies the team in the lodge minivan to the village of Omarakana, which has been the seat of power for the Tabalu lineage, from which come the Paramount Chiefs, for several hundred years. The team gazes out at a flat coral atoll largely covered by brush and crops. Kiriwina's jungles, it appears, have been severely reduced for agriculture, and its once abundant ebony trees have largely been cut by carvers, who ship their bowls and statues to dealers in Port Moresby.

Yet the land is still lush with flowering plants and fruit trees. Like much of Papua New Guinea, it remains a tropical hothouse. During the rainy season, from January to March, there is rain every day, nearly all day. In the drier season, it rains nearly every night. Mixed with equatorial solar energy, the moisture produces a perpetually green landscape.

The minivan passes men carrying freshly picked bananas and mangoes, women balancing water buckets on their heads, children with parrots on their shoulders and red hibiscus flowers behind their ears. In one village, they see women with shaved heads. A sign of mourning, Jerome explains.

The Cousteau team asks about the stories of sexual permissiveness in the Trobriands. Jerome smiles and nods. In July, during the annual yam harvest, young island women become sexually aggressive. Girls who would normally turn their faces away in shyness begin to stand along the roadway, trying to touch passing men. They scheme together, waylaying certain men and gang-raping them. The victim may be someone they dislike, in which case the rape is malicious, or someone they find fetching. They are small, Jerome laughs, but they are strong and they can scramble through the brush quickly and they spring their plot on a man when he is alone in the bush.

Changing subjects, Jerome begins to prepare the team for their encounter with the Paramount Chief. He may ask for money, Jerome says. Richards asks if he should attempt to bargain with the Chief. "No," says Jerome, "you bargain with a wood carver. You do not bargain with the Paramount Chief."

It is important, he acknowledges, that he himself do nothing to displease the Chief. To explain, he tells the story of a chief's nephew who had obtained a valued Kula necklace. Tradition dictated that he pass it along to his uncle the Chief. To do otherwise was to imply that he was the equal of his exalted leader, a spectacular *faux pas*. When he failed to release the necklace to his uncle, he was poisoned. "It was to be expected," shrugs Jerome.

A poisoning takes place in three stages. Surreptitiously injected into his food, the first dose makes the victim slightly sick, so that he assumes the cause is natural. The second dose is stronger and reveals to the victim that his end is planned for, unavoidable, and near. There passes a period of regret on the part of the victim. Then the third dose finishes him off. Such an execution can be ordered by the Paramount Chief, or virtually any village chief, and it raises no protests. It is an accepted exercise of authority.

With this briefing in mind, the team is prepared to be exceedingly serious and fair in their dealings with the Paramount Chief, who turns out to be not a scowling, wild-eyed potentate but a gentle, middle-aged bald man with a neat moustache, western slacks, and a flowered shirt.

The current Paramount Chief is introduced as Pulayasi. Every member of the Cousteau team is introduced in turn, and a quarter of an hour passes in light banter among the Chief, Jerome, and village elders seated at the Chief's side. Eventually, Jerome grows serious, and asks Richards to explain to the Chief the reason for the presence of these outsiders. The speech by Richards is translated for the Chief, who sits expressionless for a few minutes, then whispers to Jerome. The Chief asks for a fee of 400 kina, roughly $400. There is no opportunity for discussion.

And there is another thing, Jerome says. Chief Pulayasi has learned that a village chief was treated to a helicopter ride by Braunbeck and Prezelin

Papua New Guinea is largely a male-dominated realm. Women commonly perform heavy work, toting on their heads loads of yams, thatching leaves, banana bunches, or laundry. Ironically, however, Trobriand society is matrilineal—the powers of a chief pass not to his son but to his oldest nephew on his wife's side of the family.

the day before. The implication is that the Paramount Chief should be offered a ride as well. Richards asks whether the Cousteau helicopter can pick Pulayasi up one afternoon in the coming week. A wide smile serves as the answer.

During the next few days, the film team wanders from village to village on Kiriwina. They document the craft of wood carving, the harvesting of yams. They visit an island school on a day when children are obliged to wear traditional clothing and study the ways of their ancestors. They drive to Kadinaka Beach, an empty and stunning strip of white sand on the east coast of the island where, they are told, a giant grouper lives just offshore in a lagoon.

Chuck Davis dons mask, snorkel, and fins and swims about 150 yards out to the spot identified by a local man. He does not find the grouper, but when he passes through a narrow channel leading from the lagoon to the open sea, he is greeted suddenly by about twenty dolphins. The mammals approach him, look him up and down, linger for a few moments, then swim away. The scene is spectacular, with rays of sun hanging through the water ceiling like party decorations, with backlighting that gives an ethereal quality to the setting. It is everything an underwater photographer dreams of encountering one day.

But this afternoon, because he is merely scouting, Davis has elected not to carry a camera with him. For the next two days he laments his misfortune and imagines the pictures he missed. "Unquestionably a poster," he says.

On the tiny island of Muwa off the southwest coast of Kiriwina, villagers clean sea cucumbers gathered offshore by free divers, who may bring in more than six thousand a day. After they are cooked and dried in the sun, the cucumbers—not vegetables but relatives of sea stars—will be distributed throughout the Orient, where they are considered a seafood delicacy.

Chong Hin, manager of the seafood operation on Muwa Island, shows Cousteau writer-producer Mose Richards his finished product—thousands of boiled and sun-dried sea cucumbers. His cost is three dollars per kilo; a single sea cucumber will bring about thirty dollars in a Singapore or Hong Kong market.

When *Calypso* has not returned on the expected day, Richards goes to the District office in Losuia, where there is a shortwave radio. It is the only means of communication with the outside world from Kiriwina, and it is made available to the public during two three-hour periods each day. As he waits in line to have his call placed to Karen Brazeau in Port Moresby, he asks an employee of the District office if there are any plans to bring telephones to the Trobriands. There are, he is told. In fact, the equipment is all sitting in a warehouse on the mainland. But the system may never be finished because it requires a dish transmitter, which must be installed atop a mountain on Goodenough Island. But the clan that owns the mountain refuses access to it.

Such obstinate independence from the central and district governments, the man says, is a continual headache for his office. He tells a story of his attempts to introduce democratic procedures on Kiriwina. At village meetings, his officers explain various issues to be decided, then ask for the village to vote by a show of hands. Invariably, the village chief is seated at the rear of the assemblage. When the vote is called, the villagers turn to watch the Chief. When he raises his hand, they all raise theirs.

After lunch one afternoon, the team sets out for Omarakana to give Paramount Chief Pulayasi his helicopter ride. Bill Rudd and Jerome have suggested that a trip to Kitava Island would greatly please the Chief. He is anxious to learn what the Kitava men have brought back from Iwa on their Kula trip.

The trip begins in an open field next to the village, amid a squealing, pointing crowd of the Chief's family and fellow villagers. He is belted in. The crowds are directed back from the aircraft. They wave, he waves, *Felix* lifts off.

And suddenly, in this special circumstance, the mystique of the great
Paramount Chief of Kiriwina evaporates. Now he is merely a first-time
passenger in an odd-looking craft and the "Paramount Chief" of that craft
is Bob Braunbeck. Pulayasi defers, asks questions timidly, expresses his
great respect for Bob's knowledge and command of the helicopter, and
obeys Bob's every direction.

The 25-minute flight is uneventful, and the helicopter sets down at the
main village of Kitava, where another excited crowd waits. The seat belt is
unfastened, the headphones hung on the hook in the center of the cockpit,
and Pulayasi steps down onto the floats, then the ground. Immediately, his
bearing straightens, his attitude grows more serious and regal, and he
leaves Braunbeck behind. The king of the air is merely a white commoner
on the ground; the meek passenger in the sky assumes the authority
derived from his royal lineage the instant he is returned to the soil of a
Trobriand island.

On the day before *Calypso* arrives to pick up the Land Team, Rudd and
Jerome drive them to a village in the southern part of Kiriwina called

Sinaketa. Several village men have recently returned from Kitava with Kula items, and the Chief, Uwelasi, has let it be known that there will be a feast this afternoon at which their take can be viewed. As they park at the edge of Sinaketa, Rudd tells the team to wait while he asks permission for their visit. Prezelin has purchased two notebook-sized cakes of tobacco in the local store, a gift generally expected of visitors. Village men share the tobacco, rolling it into newsprint cigarettes. Prezelin gives the tobacco to Rudd, who disappears into the village.

Since the day is oppressively hot and humid, the team wanders down to the shore. They watch two dozen children at play in the gentle surf, entranced by their good looks. The normally black, bushy hair of each child has been bleached a rusty blonde color by the combination of sea salt and sun. The effect, combined with their nut-brown bodies, gives them a golden appearance.

The team is invited to meet the elders, arriving in time to catch the end of a bombastic performance by an old man who is belittling Rudd. The expat translates as the tirade continues: "Why should we allow this bastard to look at our *bagi*, when he has never treated us properly? When he has fine *bagi* or *mwali*, does he send them to us? No! He is not our friend and we should not let this traitor near our new *bagi!*" Rudd smiles, the villagers laugh.

With the obligatory harangue finished, Rudd is welcomed, and he climbs up to sit cross-legged on the bamboo and palm-leaf platform of the men's central hut. Before him lie many of the new *bagi*, and as he examines them, the team asks more questions about the Kula phenomenon.

"Imagine a club that collects something of value," he says, "such as stamps or baseball cards. Neither of these things has much intrinsic value, yet to collectors some items are precious, famous, greatly coveted. In the Kula Ring, some pieces have gained more stature than others, perhaps because of the fine quality of their shells or the design, perhaps just because they have acquired a certain renown by circulating for a long time through various well-known collectors. The man who holds these famous pieces shares some of their power and prestige."

As the afternoon passes, people from all over Kiriwina arrive to view the *bagi*, eventually joined by a beloved chief called Narubutau, a Kula master, and Paramount Chief Pulayasi himself. Gradually the center of Sinaketa fills with yam pens, mounds of food—fish, bananas, sugar-cane, vegetable stews—and the inevitable heaps of betel nuts. Several village men string two fifty-foot lines across the area and hang all of the new *bagi* from them. The team counts more than two hundred necklaces, each of which is closely inspected by the arriving visitors. Rudd points to a few prized pieces, with names like Yakiyakiba and Monikiniki. He is disappointed not to find an awaited piece called Yo-Ya.

At 4:00 P.M., Chief Uwelasi gives a speech honoring the men who have returned with such a trove. At this point, it is expected that he will begin distributing the *bagi* to their rightful holders, some of whom have come here from other parts of the island. Instead, he asks them to wait for several weeks, and the result is a long and ardent series of speeches protesting this decision. Though outright hostility does not erupt, it is clear that a certain tension is in the air. Rudd, having spent the afternoon closely studying every new *bagi*, offers the opinion that they shouldn't be so upset because the collection of items brought back by the Sinaketa men was rather inferior anyway.

Returning in the minivan, the Cousteau team reflects on what they've seen. While there are no wars, no extraordinary fighting among the islanders involved in Kula, life in the Trobriands does reveal undercurrents of violence. People who displease a chief are poisoned. A District police officer was recently stoned by angered villagers in Losuia when he attempted to remove some passengers from an overloaded bus. Rapes seem to be an accepted part of the culture. Traditional social pressures limit most crime, Jerome tells them, because the culprit is ostracized. Since the people have little regard for the District officers or their police, the only universal, final authority rests with the Paramount Chief, and the only serious punishment ever meted out is death, by poison or sorcery.

Intrigued by the Kula Ring and its peaceful dynamic in a society with subsurface violence, Didier Noirot has an idea. He reminds the team that they have a *bagi* necklace on *Calypso*, that was purchased on Rossel Island. Could that *bagi* become part of the Kula Ring? And would Rudd help the team organize that? Indeed he will, says Rudd. He will outfit it with the necessary accessories and will act as its sponsor so that it will move throughout the Kula Ring for years to come. "It will need a name," someone says. "That's obvious," says Rudd. "We'll call it 'Calypso.'"

And so it is that two days later, when *Calypso* has anchored along the western shore of Kiriwina, a party of crew members sets out by Zodiac, then transfers to the minivan, and arrives at Omarakana bearing an elaborate new *bagi*. Following instructions from Jerome and Rudd, the Cousteau entourage walks slowly to the hut of Paramount Chief Pulayasi, who sits staring straight ahead in mock disdain. Maupiti carries "Ca-

In the Kiriwina Island village of Sinaketa, men wearing the traditional male skirts called *laplaps* inspect more than 200 *bagi* necklaces recently brought back by village men on a Kula Ring trading expedition. (The structure behind them is a yam storage house.) Perhaps hoping to distinguish his *bagi*, the maker of the necklace hanging at center substituted a broken 45-rpm record for the customary mother-of-pearl shell.

On the day of their departure from Kiriwina Island, Cousteau crew members enter the village of Omarakana to present Paramount Chief Pulayasi with the newly finished *bagi* named "Calypso." From left: divers Antoine Rosset, Thierry Dupisson, Teriihaunui (Maupiti) Loyat (carrying the necklace), assistant cameraman Raymond Amaddio (head seen at the rear), and Captain Albert Falco ("Chief" of *Calypso*).

lypso," the necklace, hanging from a spear. Diver Thierry Dupisson walks alongside blowing a conch shell in the manner of a trumpet, though, in the case of the unpracticed Dupisson, it sounds more like a tire going flat. Assorted deckhands and divers straggle at the sides, and in the place of honor comes the Chief of *Calypso*, Albert Falco.

Bebert launches into a stirring denunciation of his new Kula partner. Such an undistinguished character, even if he is a Paramount Chief, is surely not entitled to this magnificent *bagi*, which is carried here by a scientific expedition that has toured the entire globe and has filmed the most extraordinary things. Pulayasi bats away a fly, but otherwise remains frozen in disregard. Whereupon, as Jerome has suggested, Maupiti throws the spear and trailing necklace so that it sticks into the wall of the Chief's hut. No response. The Cousteau team waits patiently, hoping they have followed the appropriate custom. At last, Pulayasi turns to a man at his side. "Take this pathetic *bagi* and show it to the women," he says scornfully. "Perhaps it will amuse them."

Thus, a Kula necklace named "Calypso" enters the legendary Kula Ring of the Solomon Sea on April 21, 1988. It is destined to travel along the Kula route, perhaps for ten years or longer, and to remind islanders of the white ship that ventured through. It would be interesting, the team decides, to return in ten years and find out what its travels have been . . . and whether it is a piece of great acclaim or just another mediocre *bagi* compared to the illustrious Yakiyakiba, Monikiniki, and Yo-Ya.

THE MELANESIAN
WILD WEST

We were brought

up fighting,

fighting is like

food to us.

John Waiko, in

The Unexpected Hawk

Though Asaros today
don mud masks only
for ceremonial dances,
the ancestors of this
man used the
fearsome disguises to
frighten neighboring
villagers.

J.-M. C.: While Calypso *explores islands enveloped in tropical serenity and peaceable rituals, my father and I send our Land Team into a world of richer earth and darker emotions. They will follow in the steps of the first humans who settled in Papua New Guinea some 50,000 years ago, climbing from the lowland jungles that frame the country into the broad cordillera that runs through its center like a backbone.*

Like our expedition, the first explorers must have arrived by watercraft. The sea crossings from Asia would have been shorter then, since the shallower Ice Age seas were broken by larger island masses. To the south, in fact, New Guinea and Australia were joined by lands now submerged beneath the Torres Strait.

In the upland valleys of the central mountains the new arrivals found a secluded homeland of exceptional fertility. Material disgorged from Pleistocene volcanoes and eroded from their steep slopes after quiescence had accumulated in great intermontane beds of humic brown ash. Though these broad valley floors were at high altitudes, they were irrigated by a warm and wet equatorial climate with no marked dry season. The volcanic ash weathered to deep, organically rich topsoil.

With such a productive land beneath them, the settlers of Papua New Guinea's Highlands soon became some of the world's first gardeners. They gradually burned and cut native oaks, beeches, laurels, and pines, replacing them with edible native foods they could cultivate: bananas, yams, sugarcane, peanuts, breadfruit, coconuts, pandanus, wild almonds, and sago. So extensive were their conversions of existing forest land into gardens and grasslands that today, although three-quarters of Papua New Guinea is still forested, the central Highlands retain dense tree cover only along the highest bordering mountains and ridges.

Naturally, the abundance of food allowed human numbers to grow, making these high plateaus of Papua New Guinea the largest population centers in all of the Pacific islands. Yet, initially, the expanding clans and villages that would eventually total nearly a million people were largely isolated from one another by the height and complexity of the mountain walls surrounding them. Mount Wilhelm, the country's highest peak, is a hundred feet higher than the Matterhorn. Imagine the obstacles presented by a range like the Alps, blanketed with jungle and muddied by as much as fifteen feet of rain annually. The maze of forested crests and ridges effectively boxed the early settlers in, so that each valley or canyon became the birthplace of a new culture with a new language or dialect.

As villages grew and territories butted against one another, the potential for conflict increased. The result has been tens of thousands of years of enmity and sporadic violence between some neighboring groups and fascinating cultural mechanisms to regulate these volatile tensions.

Though only a half-century has passed since many Highlanders were first discovered by the outside world, the steady influx of missionaries and material civilization has tempered much of their violence. But not all of it. Foreign doctors working for short periods at Highland medical stations still go home to Europe or America with extraordinary tales—about the scores of villagers who show up each weekend seeking medical attention for critical arrow wounds; about warriors engaged in fierce bow-and-arrow battles who stop briefly to allow carloads of tourists to pass by on the road between them, then resume trying to kill one another; about the Cessna that took off from an airstrip with the pilot and passengers ducking as arrows and spears sailed past during an exchange between two enemy groups lining either side of the runway.

The government of Papua New Guinea tries to dissuade visiting journalists and anthropologists from drawing attention to Highland violence, under-

standably angered that such coverage sketches an unfair international image of the country and ignores its formidable democratic and cultural accomplishments. For a country trying to build up tourism, rumors of a dangerous countryside roamed by "savages" can be catastrophic.

As the Cousteau Land Team arrives in the coastal town of Lae, prepared to set out into the Highlands, the advance information portrays a world greatly pacified by modern changes. Even where squabbles develop among people in the mountains, they are told, outsiders are almost never drawn into the mayhem. This is a world, after all, where pedestrians along the roadside can be seen on occasion wearing baseball caps and listening to portable radios.

And yet, when they arrange for the rental of two vehicles to carry them through the mountains, the agent in Lae is very careful to warn them never to drive after dark. That simply is not done, and especially by foreigners carrying expensive equipment. One could hit a pedestrian or a pig, igniting some unpleasantness among the local people. Very complicated. Why risk the danger? ("Danger" is "samting nogut" in Pidgin). The expedition gets under way with a little trepidation, and a lot of curiosity.

On March 7th, the Land Team sets out in two four-wheel-drive, four-door pickups. Expedition Leader Don Santee has carried several Cousteau Society emblems—the Calypso maiden and dolphin—from the Los Angeles office. As gear is being packed into the truck beds, diver Marc Blessington affixes the adhesive-backed rubber logos onto the doors of the pickups. It is a symbolic act, like painting the name on a newly finished vessel. The expedition is launched.

Driving westward out of Lae onto the Highland Highway the team is lighthearted, in part because the adventure is finally commencing, in part because the team is composed of friends who have worked together in far-flung corners of the world. A winsome humor percolates just below the surface, fueled by the wry observations of Santee, a veteran diver with the savvy and versatile skills required of expedition leaders, and the droll wit of sound engineer Gary Holland, a buoyant spirit from Louisiana who first joined the Cousteau team as it explored the Mississippi. Their humor is shared by still photographer Anne-Marie Cousteau, who has learned to look with amusement upon uncomfortable situations in remote places, and Blessington, whose mixed French and British background produces both surface propriety and subtle comedy.

The driving force during the weeks ahead, however, will be cinematographer Jean-Paul Cornu, who can be impish in his off hours but is bursting with solemn intensity as he directs the film work. Cornu's formidable talents, honed by his years of work in the French cinema, have enriched Cousteau films from the Nile to the Amazon to the South Pacific.

The newest team member, Papua New Guinea national Martin Medan, will spend the first few days quietly observing his associates, learning the ropes. Medan comes from Rabaul but is currently a film student at the *Skul Bilong Wokim Piksa* in Goroka. He has joined the team to act as Cornu's camera assistant, as well as guide and translator.

A few miles outside of Lae, the two trucks turn south on a road that twists and turns up into the hills. The plan is to explore the area around the towns of Wau and Bulolo, where a gold rush in the 1920s and 1930s attracted thousands of foreigners and initiated the opening of the Highlands to the outside world.

After metamorphosis, this caterpillar will emerge from a cocoon as one of Papua New Guinea's most celebrated forms of wildlife, a bird-wing butterfly.

A bird-wing butterfly pauses on a hibiscus flower. Bird-wings are the best known of Papua New Guinea's hundreds of butterfly varieties: among the group is the world's largest butterfly, the Queen Alexandria's bird-wing, which is found only here.

The first stop is near Bulolo, where the team is treated to its first glimpse of the lush beauty of the interior rain forests of Papua New Guinea. They visit a farm run by a former Sepik Province agriculture officer, Australian Peter Clark. His crop is not the vines he cultivates in long rows but the butterfly cocoons attached to them.

Unlike the broad savannahs of Africa, which support herds of large animals, rain forests around the world are principally kingdoms of the small and the microscopic. The lack of open space and grasses for grazing limits the size of jungle creatures, and the most spectacular inhabitants are often tree dwellers, such as birds and insects. Papua New Guinea is no exception. The three dozen species of birds of paradise found here may be the most beautiful birds in the world. These long-plumed and timid creatures are treasured symbols, appearing on everything from the national flag and currency to the logos of practically every commercial product that originates in Papua New Guinea. Bird of paradise feathers are components of the traditional decorative outfits worn in villages throughout the country.

Yet the hundreds of species of lepidoptera fluttering through the forests of Papua New Guinea may exceed in exotic beauty and brilliance even the birds of paradise. They include both the world's largest butterfly, the Queen Alexandra's birdwing, and the world's largest moth, the atlas moth.

The butterfly farm near Bulolo has been established to turn these dazzling creatures into a new cash crop for Papua New Guinea and to protect them from extinction as well. Clark gives Don Santee a tour of the operation, shows him cocoons fastened to leaves, and adult butterflies that remain within the bounds of the open-air farm, more attracted to Clark's carefully selected host vines than to the surrounding woods.

Though many of the butterflies originate on the grounds, Clark also has a network of a thousand Highlanders who raise the creatures in their own gardens, or find them in the forest, and send cocoons and adults to him. He tells Santee that his butterfly crops are sold to dealers, who in turn send the creatures to collectors and manufacturers in Europe, North America, and Japan, which is the world leader in butterfly commerce. About ninety percent of the insects will eventually reach collectors. The rest will go to museums and producers of butterfly-adorned products, ranging from furniture and jewelry to bookmarkers.

Some idea of the size of the Papua New Guinea butterflies can be gained from this species perched on a hut wall. (Photograph by David Gillison)

In his office, Clark points to scores of framed butterflies, explaining that some of the species are critically endangered, among them the Queen Alexandra's birdwing, which inhabits only a small territory. As human populations expand here, butterfly habitats are gradually receding with the increase in slash-and-burn agriculture. Projected commercial forestry operations would further jeopardize the insects. The strategy of Clark and other butterfly farmers is to encourage nationals to see the creatures as a potential money-making crop, to develop a local appreciation for the species' well being, and to build, in the process, a base for local employment and entrepreneurial profit that is harmonious with forest conservation.

After a night in Bulolo, the Cousteau team heads higher into the mountains toward the town of Wau, where they spend the next five days combing the adjacent hills to detail on film the area of the interior first penetrated by foreigners. It was here, in 1921, that a renowned prospector named "Sharkeye" Park struck gold and sparked a massive gold rush. (Legends about Park abound, including one about the novel way he used his glass eye. When leaving his mine for a bout of drinking in Bulolo, he would remove the eye, set it on a rock, and tell his native workers he would be keeping an eye on them to be certain they kept working in his absence. The ploy succeeded until one clever workman had the idea of covering the eye with his hat as soon as Park left.)

Workers attempt to repair equipment used in the gold mining operation run by French prospectors Jacques and Joseph Da Costa along the Bulolo River. Today, though some mines take steps to protect the environment, mines like that of the Da Costas often dump toxic wastes directly into adjacent rivers.

An infant tree kangaroo practices his trade. (Photograph by David Gillison)

Arriving prospectors were introduced immediately to the difficulties presented by Papua New Guinea's climate and terrain. To reach the gold site from the coast, they had to climb for eight days through entangling jungle and up steep, muddy slopes. Today, though a serpentine dirt road meanders through the hills around Wau, travel can still be difficult. Steady rains loosen hillsides, triggering landslides that can block traffic for hours or days. In some places, mud pools in the roadway are nearly impassable.

But the weather holds for the Cousteau team during their first days of travel. The first stop is at a mine run by an Australian firm called New Guinea Goldfields Limited, where Santee interviews mine manager Philip Winn. For the most part, the easily extracted alluvial deposits of gold around Wau and Bulolo were exhausted by the beginning of World War II, and prospectors migrated to other parts of the country. The production that remains is relatively meager, and must be accomplished by heavy industrial equipment in order to retrieve profitable amounts of gold. Winn says that his operation recovers only two grams of gold in each ton of rock—less than two parts per million.

As Cornu and Santee tour the mine, they discover that huge vats of cyanide are used to leach the embedded gold from crushed rocks. They wonder if this poison is reaching the Bulolo River. Winn tells them that the mine owners try very hard to isolate wastes in holding ponds and that their runoff of heavy metals and toxic substances is only half of the World Health Organization standards.

Winn is quick to point out the measures they have taken to make the mine acceptable. Of three hundred employees, only ten are expatriates. They have a testing program to find suitable trees for reforestation of the land when the mine eventually closes. And as for the future of the local people, he believes the skills they have developed working at the mine will be useful even when the mine is gone.

J.-M. C.: As our team leaves, Jean-Paul decides to seek opinions about the mining from the traditional owners of the land here, the local villagers. With the help of Gutz Schwefurth, an advisor to the Premier of Morobe Province, the team finds a national who has acted as a spokesman for villagers in negotiations with the mining concern. Since Papua New Guinea recognizes the claims of its traditional societies to the lands hunted and farmed for centuries around their villages, foreigners who would exploit the country's mineral resources must, in theory at least, come to terms with the rightful owners before they can dig a spade of earth.

Our team drives to a village north of Wau, where Ben Joseph greets them and takes them on a tour of the houses occupied by his clan, which numbers twenty-five immediate family members and an extended family of two hundred. Joseph has helped to secure shares for his people in the nearby commercial gold mine, and they now receive cash payments regularly.

He tells Don Santee of the difficulties he faces in his dealings with the mine. One problem is that the villages in the surrounding area are ancient foes. Yet before he can negotiate with the mines, every village must concur in the position he will take. After centuries of killing one another, traditional enemies suddenly find themselves sharing common problems that can only be solved with a unified front. It is tremendously difficult, says Joseph.

But the greater challenge is somehow to control wisely the changing lifestyles. Joseph says he is of two minds about the arrival of foreign prospectors in their midst. On the one hand, development is altering their environment, so that it is more difficult to find the traditional gifts of nature—game and native vegetables to eat and wood to build with, for example. On the other hand, they can now go to a store to buy these things. They don't have to go through the rigors of hunting; they can purchase "tin fish"—canned seafood such as tuna that has become ubiquitous in developing regions of the country.

Asked what will happen when the mine closes, Joseph says he hopes the land can be planted with coffee or commercial timber. Though he reveres the old ways, and ponders how to preserve them, he also admits that he himself would like to buy a corrugated metal roof for his house, and dreams of riding in a car rather than walking. Then again, he says shaking his head, are any of these advances worth it if the mine pollutes the village drinking water and harms the children?

As our team wanders about the village, they note a duality of conditions: a mother picking lice from the head of her baby sits on the porch of a house constructed not from bamboo and palm leaves but planed lumber; another mother is fastening store-bought diapers on her baby, a young girl weaves a traditional bilum *bag while her sister in the background is washing plastic dishes.*

In time-honored fashion, an independent miner pans and sluices gold from the Bulolo River near Wau. The flakes he collects will be sold to a large commercial operation upriver, giving the miner enough cash to sustain his family and the mining company a free scouring service to catch flecks it would otherwise miss.

As they drive away, the Land Team discusses the enigmas facing both Highlanders and foreign businesses. Although there are cultural complications and environmental abuses in the mining situation here, local leaders like Ben Joseph seem deeply aware of the implications for his people's future, and the mine operators seem aware at least that their operation must make concessions to its neighbors. But two days later, the team visits a working gold mine marked by insensitivity and greed.

Brothers Jacques and Joseph da Costa have come to Papua New Guinea from Ariege in the southwest of France. Experienced gold miners, they have worked a variety of sites before settling on a hillside along the Bulolo River below Wau. Though Joseph has been in the country only two years, Jacques has spent sixteen years here. In 1980, he found gold on the site of his present mine. But government restrictions against the purchase of land by foreigners left him frustrated. Jacques found a loophole in the law. In an act of capitalistic hubris, he married a woman from the village that owned the property. Now, since he was related to a landowner, he was able to establish his mine.

Because gold is sparse here, they must process a great deal of rock to make a profit sizable enough to justify the effort. Jacques's wife has title to about twenty-five acres of land, which includes a hill at the convergence of the Bulolo and one of its tributaries. The plan is to completely level the hill, in hopes of netting at least a gram of gold per ton.

"If there is a million tons of rock here," says Joseph, "we'll come away with a million grams of gold, and that's enough to live on." (About fourteen million U.S. dollars as gold prices stand that day.)

In their conversations with Marc Blessington, it soon becomes apparent that the Da Costa brothers are unconcerned about the effects of the mine on the local environment. If carried to fruition, their plan to level the hill will severely alter the nature of the Bulolo River, which flows on past scores of Highland villages. Moreover, their process employs mercury, which forms an amalgam with gold and simplifies its extraction. The waste mercury is dumped directly into the river system, which supplies the drinking water for thousands of people downstream.

Since Jacques opened the mine, however, a new Minister of Mines had taken office, and the two brothers are worried that he may soon crack down. In the meantime, employing local workers at $20 per week, they intend to accumulate as much gold as they can.

"And what then?" asks Blessington.

"Very simple," says Jacques. "I plan to retire in three years and move to Australia, where most of my profits have been invested or deposited in banks."

The next day, as the team drives the backroads near Bulolo, they spot an abandoned gold dredge on a hillside above the road. They park the two trucks and spend an hour examining and filming the dredge. They recall reading that the prospectors of sixty years ago, faced with the need to transport their mining gear into these roadless wilds, hired pilots to fly the mammoth pieces of equipment from Lae in Junker trimotors. In fact, so much material passed through Lae in the 1930s that it was one of the busiest airports in the world on the basis of freight tonnage. In 1937, it gained another kind of fame. On her round-the-world flight, aviatrix Amelia Earhart took off eastward from Lae for tiny Howland Island and was never seen again.

Returning to their trucks, the team discovers that someone has broken in, rifled through their belongings in apparent haste, and made off with several cassette tapes, Anne-Marie's camera bag, and some of Blessington's clothing. Recognizing that the world they have entered demands not only cautionary driving but a certain vigilance over personal belongings, they return to Lae vowing to keep a close watch on their expedition equipment.

In streams like this one between the villages of Wau and Bulolo, Australian prospectors discovered gold in the early 1920s, igniting an era more renowned for the challenges of harsh terrain, tropical diseases, and hostile local villagers than for yields of precious metal.

Morning fog veils a hillside above the village of Angapina. Pockets of mist and fog commonly linger in Highland valleys long after moisture has disappeared from surrounding ridges and peaks.

The "Smoked Warriors of Aseki" still sit atop scaffolding some eighty years after the attack that killed them. The bamboo and black palm arrows that killed them still lodge where they entered the bodies. Once each year, villagers of Angapina reverentially daub red ocher clay on the remaining skin to preserve it, giving the figures their color.

In an area to the east of Wau called Aseki, high in a mountain pocket walled by huge buttresses of limestone, the team finds their attention diverted from things exploitive to things eerie. They drive to the tiny village of Angapina, in the territory once ruled by the Kukukuku people — who now lead a peaceful existence but were once notorious for their ferocity. Small in stature, often less than five feet tall, they nevertheless carried out violent raids on villages in the valleys below, then repaired back to their mountain fortress. Many wore necklaces of human bones and were famed for their machine-gun-like speed at firing arrows. Today, their descendants prefer to be known as the Angas, since the word Kukukuku means "thieves."

With Martin's help, the team finds an elder of Angapina named Mbuka, who agrees for a small price to guide them to a site seldom visited by foreigners. High on a hill behind the village, in a protected alcove formed by overhanging limestone, more than a dozen human figures sit in startlingly lifelike positions, their skeletons loosely draped in orange skin, their bone faces locked in the vacant stares of the mummified.

Mbuka tells the story in Pidgin, and Martin translates. Some eighty years ago, the village was attacked by a hostile neighboring tribe. Several Kukukuku men, and two women carrying babies, lost their lives heroically defending the village. So moved were the rest of the Kukukukus that they

The smoked body on the right is that of a Kukukuku woman, one of two who died alongside men in the legendary attack by enemy villagers. Both women hold the skeletons of children in their laps, as if still shielding them after eighty years.

decided to pay homage by smoking the lifeless bodies to preserve them and placing them like mythical statues on a ledge above the village. There, they would always be remembered, and their deeds would be a continuing source of inspiration.

For the Cousteau team, it is a haunting introduction to the violence that has reverberated through the Highlands for millenia.

On March 15th, the team drives northwest for four hours to the port city of Madang, where they spend two days inquiring about, and briefly visiting, a huge forestry operation called JANT (Japanese—Australian—Niugini Timber), which is run by a Japanese company. Torrential rains, however, soon make the roads at the project impassable, and Cornu decides to postpone the filming at JANT until later. They return halfway back to Lae, then turn west and follow the Highland Highway to Goroka.

Now a town of 12,000 people, and a center of commerce for the central Highlands area, Goroka was one of the first outposts established by Australian administrators when they moved to open up the interior of the Mandated Territory of New Guinea in the 1930s. The Australian patrol officers sent to pacify the countryside (called "Kiaps" by the nationals) found a rough and often bloody world when they ventured into the mountains from Goroka. To the southeast of Goroka, for example, they discovered a curious disease called Kuru, which seemed to center around the village of Okapa. Kuru victims died as the disease attacked their central nervous system, and because they often had an odd smile on their faces at the time of death, it was called the laughing disease. At first puzzled by its origin, visiting outsiders eventually concluded that it was a result of ritual cannibalism of the dead. (Although cases of Kuru are still reported, there are said to be less than ten a year.)

Men in the Highland village of Komuniva begin the lengthy process of preparing for a Mudman dance, one of the most spectacular rites in Papua New Guinea.

To demonstrate their techniques, Asaro dancers fashioned this mask for the Cousteau Film Team. A burlap hood is coated with clay and the mask is modeled to fit the dancer.

But for sheer otherworldly spectacle and the trappings of cultural violence, none of the exotic peoples discovered by the Australians could match the legendary Asaro Mudmen. Wearing ghostly, pumpkin-sized clay masks, coated in pale mud, they presented a horrific specter that had long intimidated the other tribes of the region.

To visit these famed warriors, the Cousteau team drives to a village near Goroka called Komuniva, one of thirteen villages where nearly 3,000 people are united by the Asaro language. Komuniva is divided in two by the road. One side seems characterized by an older population and weathered huts, the other side by young families amid a setting of neat thatched cottages, expansive lawns, and rows of poinsettia bushes.

In the center of a dirt clearing in the older section of Komuniva, an elderly man is blowing a gourd horn. The team learns that the notorious village of warriors is being called to Sunday morning church services. When the gourd trumpeter finishes, another villager picks up a stone, walks to a bamboo and palm-leaf church, and begins clanging the church bell, which is in fact a steel automobile wheel suspended from a wire. Gradually the tiny church fills up, the service begins, and the Cousteau team's first vision of the Mudmen is that of about two dozen or so pious Christian men sitting with their wives and children listening to a priest.

When the church service is finished, the village pours out and invites the team to cross the road and watch dancers dress in the newer part of the village for a Mudman dance later in the day. While the preparation is under way, Marc Blessington learns that some of the village elders recall the days when Mudmen in full regalia made murderous attacks on neighboring villages. Moreover, they were present during that dramatic moment when a white man first walked into their midst.

Blessington is introduced by the village leader, Ruipo Gumio, to his father, Atairo Kanisuo, and an awkward interview begins. Blessington asks questions in English, which are translated by Martin Medan into Pidgin, then translated by Ruipo Gumio into Asaro, the only language spoken by the old man. Kanisuo's answers, of course, must travel back through a reverse circuit of translations.

"Before, when we had enemies at war with us," he says, "the people of this village would wear mud masks because it disguised them. We could attack a village and kill without being recognized. People thought we were ghosts and they would flee us. In their mud disguises, our men chased the enemies, cutting off heads, burning down houses, and slaughtering pigs. Then we would return home and hide our masks. They believed ghosts were responsible. They didn't know it was our villagers."

Kanisuo waves his arm toward Cornu and Holland, who are filming the preparations for the dance. "Now you will film and you may think there is nothing to this. Just a strange dance. But this was not a joking matter. Not at all. This was something that struck terror into people. And the Mudmen destroyed thousands of people. And the feasting that followed these attacks was huge."

"What made the Asaro stop this practice?" Blessington asks.

"When the missionaries came we gave up a lot of our traditions," says Kanisuo, "but we held on to the tradition of the mud masks. We don't use them for killing. Just for dancing. Just for dancing. We wanted to keep some of our fathers' traditions."

Although contact with whites is no longer a unique event for the Asaro, the appearance of a white woman wearing pants, working alongside men, and operating complicated gadgets seems to fascinate the village women.

They watch Anne-Marie closely all day, staring at her long pants in puzzlement. Occasionally, a bold woman will reach out to touch her skin or hair.

As the team is preparing to leave, an old woman approaches her, chasing away the children gathered in a knot around the intriguing visitor. Unsure what is about to transpire, Anne-Marie stands quietly, waiting. The woman has the stern look of someone compelled to resolve unfinished business. She puts a hand on each of Anne-Marie's arms as if to examine her muscles, then on her legs. Finally, as a conclusive test, she moves her hands to Anne-Marie's breasts. Suddenly, the old woman smiles broadly, and nods to the other village women, who are now satisfied that Anne-Marie is a female.

On March 24th, the team drives to a coffee plantation near Mount Hagen in the Wahgi Valley. Here, the first contacts between Highlanders and Europeans are recalled by an old man with a different perspective. Seventy-five-year-old Daniel Leahy was just nineteen when he joined his older brother to search for gold at a camp south of present-day Goroka. It was Michael Leahy, accompanied by Michael Dwyer, who had first discovered the vast Highland civilization only two years earlier. (Among the Australians who often traveled the mountains with Michael Leahy was James Taylor, a patrol officer who is still remembered by the Asaro as their first white friend.)

The Leahy brothers were to the Highlands what the Columbus brothers were to the West Indies. As the first and most dominant of the early white settlers here, Michael soon became, and remains after his death, something of a legend. Though his only real interest was finding gold, his wide

Some Asaro elders still recall the days when masked warriors conducted violent raids on enemy villages, burning them to the ground and killing wantonly.

excursions through the mountains made him a combination explorer, diplomat, and white master. Eventually, he was joined in his prospecting by three brothers—Patrick, James, and Daniel.

The sole survivor, Dan Leahy is now nearly blind and deaf. Yet when the Cousteau team arrives, he is eager to talk about his experiences.

When the Leahy's first visited an uncontacted village, the exchanges were invariably marked by a wariness on the part of the shocked tribes. Gifts were offered and accepted, local food traded in return. Yet on the second visit to a village, the situation changed diametrically. Since the whites had not harmed them, the confidence of the Highlanders returned. They began to suspect that the whites were weak, since they had not simply killed them and stolen their goods, as any strong people of the Highlands would likely have done.

Gradually, the villagers began to test the whites, stealing knives and axes left unattended. When the prospectors took exception and fired their rifles over the heads of the offenders, the stolen items were returned. But the mood changed. In some cases, angered warriors rushed the prospectors' camp. Concluding that their lives were in danger, the white men fired off shots to wound the attackers. When events escalated, they shot to kill.

Through the efforts of patrolmen like Taylor, many of these conflicts were quelled without bloodshed, but not all. Some prospectors, including Michael Leahy, suffered wounds from arrows or clubs. Some villagers were killed by rifle fire. It is impossible to know how many died. Some remote encounters may not have been reported by the miners, and time has blurred memories.

Dan Leahy claims that Highlanders were never shot unless they were directly threatening the life of the white men. Whatever the reality, the

Modern Mudmen simulate in dance an attack on a neighboring villager.

incidents of conflict soon faded as villagers came to understand the superiority of the white men's weapons. Moreover, they respected such strength, and with their traditional indisposition to cooperate amongst themselves, there was no chance of villages uniting to form an army and drive the white men away. As a result, Australia could manage their mandate using small patrols; they were never forced to send a standing army to Papua New Guinea.

Gradually, a kind of mutually exploitive relationship grew between the Highlanders and the prospectors. The villagers wanted things from the whites. They treasured the seashells and beads carried by white men as a kind of primitive currency, and they coveted the steel axes and knives that were so superior to their stone tools. In turn, Leahy and other prospectors needed the cooperation and help of Highlanders. They sought food from village gardens, and they solicited workers to help with the tasks of prospecting and mining.

Since the foreigners were almost universally young, single men, another need entered the picture. As the Highlanders grew comfortable with the whites, sexual liaisons occurred. In some cases, these affairs were relatively innocent. More often, sexual favors were traded by women for shells and tools, usually at the urging of their own husbands.

One such case involved a young, pretty woman named Yamka Amp Wenta. Only fifteen at the time, she was taken by her husband to a prospectors' camp three times, and offered in trade for shells, tools, and pork. One white man took a particular liking to her and paid the husband, who departed with the goods. After each visit, Wenta returned to her husband. But when several weeks had passed, it became apparent that she was pregnant. When the baby was born, the infant boy was unusually light skinned, and his hair was straighter than that of most Highlanders. The father, Wenta later confessed, was Michael Leahy.

After their visit with Daniel Leahy, the Cousteau team drives several miles to another coffee plantation. The owner, Clem Leahy, is tall, balding, and cast in the light-brown complexion produced by the union of Yamka Amp Wenta and Michael Leahy. Raised in his mother's village, Clem eventually was sent to a Catholic mission school and hired by his Uncle Daniel, who treated him like a son. Clem explains that his father was unaware for many years of his existence. Michael Leahy had eventually moved on to another part of the country and married a European woman. He never acknowledged this mixed-race child—nor two other sons born of Highland women.

Wenta, the team learns, is still alive. Cornu asks if they can meet and interview her.

White-haired, shy, nearing seventy years of age, Wenta now lives in the village of Walya near Mount Hagen. Clem accompanies the team to the village, leads them to his mother's house, and hugs her affectionately.

Wenta remembers the confusion that reigned in her village when the whites arrived. Like most Highlanders, she initially believed them to be "devils." Some people thought they were skypeople, and in one village to the west the men surreptitiously dug up the buried excrement of the whites to see if it resembled that dropped by birds.

When Santee asks Wenta about the period before the arrival of the whites, she recalls it as a time of endless hostility.

"Everybody was fighting," she says. "Some tribes were almost wiped out. There was no peace. The white man traveled everywhere, and they stopped the tribal fights."

With her child alongside, a woman cultivates tea on a Highland plantation near Mount Hagen. Once, only foreign planters raised such crops in the country, but since 1970 an increasing number of smallholders have added tea and coffee to their subsistence gardens.

J.-M. C.: Like the Leahy brothers, who found gold but never the mother lode they sought, many of the prospectors who remained in Papua New Guinea turned to coffee as a source of wealth when they abandoned the hunt for mineral riches. Patrick Leahy eventually became a millionaire, and it was he who suggested that his brother Daniel establish the coffee plantation that still supports him. Clem Leahy was able to buy a plantation when its owner left the country as Independence arrived. The planter believed that chaos would reign when nationals were in charge and that people would run about chopping each other's heads off.

The fertile valleys of the Highlands, where some of the planet's first human gardens were begun, also turned out to be ideal for growing coffee. Scores of expatriates arrived to develop coffee plantations, as well as processing and marketing operations. They taught the Highlanders how to raise coffee, and thousands of these nationals began to produce coffee beans in their own gardens, gradually replacing some of their food crops. By 1967, Highlanders sold twice as much coffee as the foreign-owned plantations. They had learned the bisnis *well.*

Earlier, in their visit to the Asaro, our team has noticed that women sit in front of many village huts, spreading coffee beans to dry in the sun. Though most of Papua New Guinea is still an economy of subsistence farmers, most of these farmers also grow a cash crop—coffee in the Highlands, cocoa, coconuts, or oil palm at lower altitudes.

Like the missions that would gradually modify the beliefs of the Highlanders, coffee and other cash crops gradually altered their lifestyles. Before the 1940s, few villagers had ever heard of money. But year by year, and village by village, their self-sufficiency gave way to a dependency on cash. Fields of sweet potato, taro, cassava, and sago palm were replaced by coffee trees. Selling coffee beans enabled them to purchase the food increasingly unavailable as subsistence gardens declined and populations grew.

It is the same shift we have observed throughout the developing world. How can we evaluate it as good or bad? On the one hand, access to money is not only inevitable but carries with it the power to obtain medicines and books and schooling for children, as well as trinkets. On the other hand, the more dependent villagers become on cash, the more they are hostages to economic systems beyond their control and the more remote they become from the natural world. They lose interest in the priceless secrets of nature long passed down by their ancestors. In the process, they are poorer for this loss of knowledge, and so are all the rest of us.

A Highland woman picks ripened coffee beans at a plantation field near Mount Hagen owned by Clem Leahy, son of Highlands explorer Michael Leahy and villager Yamka Amp Wenta. Coffee is the most important cash crop in Papua New Guinea today. It was introduced in the 1950s by outsiders, many of them gold prospectors who took advantage of the fertile ground of the Highlands and turned to farming when the low price of gold made mining less profitable after World War II. The Highland coffee crop is today one of the world's richest.

An Asaro woman spreads coffee beans to dry in the sun. The introduction of coffee production vastly changed the lives of many Highlanders, who once grew their own crops but now often raise coffee for export instead.

On March 25th, the Cousteau team drives to a village about fifteen miles from Mt. Hagen. Local people have told Cornu that a special ceremony is about to take place in Kindau, one rooted in the ancient Highland ritual called a "payback."

The idea is simple, and it resembles the Western "eye for an eye." Except that the revenge need not be so precise as that. If a man was killed by someone from another village, the clan of the victim was expected to make a reprisal raid. The goal was not necessarily to punish the culprit but his people. If avengers found the killer, fine. If not, they might kill virtually any man, woman, or child in the enemy village. To fail to make such a "payback" was probably as reprehensible in the minds of Highlanders as the original murder, maybe more so.

National leader Sir Albert Maori Kiki, who grew up in a precontact tribe, wrote of the importance of paybacks in his autobiography, *10,000 Years in a Lifetime:* "In a sense it was the war with neighboring peoples, the constant watch out for enemy activities, the 'payback' expeditions, the preparation of weapons, that provided the major content and the excitement of our lives. . . . I think we did not really want peace because we *enjoyed* the fighting."

The gradual intrusion of whites and their legal systems into the Highlands greatly reduced the number and vehemence of the old payback raids. Today, an automobile accident can spark a payback squabble, and arrows still fly on occasion, but the phenomena are pale shadows of the fiery conflicts of the past.

Among the Highland groups once famed for paybacks is a Melpa-speaking society called the Wigmen, whose name derives from elaborate headdresses woven of human hair. Though the wigs are worn exclusively by men, they are made from the hair of village women, who are consequently short-haired much of the time.

The Cousteau team spends two days filming near Kindau at a clearing that serves as a kind of fairgrounds for local rituals. Just as they arrive, it begins to rain, turning the dirt field into a sheet of mud. The team notices an old man standing alone in the middle of the clearing. He is slowly turning, looking at the sky, raising his arms, and chanting prayers. When he finishes, Santee and Cornu introduce themselves and ask what he is doing.

Women from the
village of Kindau are
adorned in their finest
costumes for the rare
"payback" feast.

Two Melpa wigmen
in the village of
Kindau begin the
"payback" ceremony
beating the traditional
drums called *kundus*.
Their headdresses are
woven of human hair
supplied by village
women. By custom,
Melpa men are
costumed to create a
"dark" effect, Melpa
women to achieve a
"bright" appearance.

It turns out that the old man, Kerua Kemnga, is the host of the affair about to begin, and he has been praying for an end to the rain. In fact, he has been calling for help from either the spirit of his dead grandfather or the Christian God.

Santee is curious. "Why both?" he asks. "Do you believe in the spirits of the ancestors, or do you believe in the God of the whites?"

"Both," says Kerua. "The ancients knew only the spirits of the ancestors, and that worked for them. The white man came and he knew a Big Man above, and that worked for him. As for me, I believe as my fathers did. But to be sure, I call them both."

Santee asks Kerua the meaning of the feast being prepared.

Some thirty years ago, in the midst of a quarrel over the ownership of a pig, Kerua lost his temper and killed a man named Maep Tep, who was from an enemy village. The death occurred during the first years of white influence in the region. Kerua, in fact, was working for Daniel Leahy at the time.

Although tradition dictated that a payback raid occur, the clan of the victim was forbidden by Australian patrol officers from carrying out such an attack, and Kerua was jailed for one month. As a result, in the minds of village elders, the death of Maep Tep was never properly dealt with. Tensions have persisted between the two villages for thirty years.

Now, Kerua and his three sons have decided to offer a peaceful compensation to the two sons of his victim, resolving a matter lingering from the old days of traditional "payback" law. Henceforth, the slate will be clean, and both villages will abide by modern law.

Through the day, people from the surrounding countryside arrive for this modern variation on a "payback," and the grounds take on the festive atmosphere of a sporting event. Women position themselves around the edges of the crowd selling peanuts, balls of dough fried in oil, and cooked vegetables. Children race about shouting or stand transfixed watching the preparations, absently chewing sugarcane. Dancers spend the entire morning applying makeup and donning the feathers, beads, shells, mud, and stalks of foliage that comprise a Wigman's regalia.

The singsing dances begin slowly, then continue vigorously for the rest of the day and evening, only to begin again on the morning of the second day and last until late in the afternoon. When the time comes at last for the ceremony, forty-two stakes are driven into the ground, and forty-two pigs—Kerua's compensation payment to Maep Tep's sons—are led to the stakes. There follows a seemingly unending procession of speakers, most of them old, who tell and retell the story of the murder, the purpose of this singsing, perhaps even the ancient history of each village.

Exhausted by the spectacle—and the continual drumbeats, the squealing pigs, and the two-day sensory feast of stunning colors and images—the Cousteau team quietly packs their gear away, expresses their gratitude to all, and leaves the singsing grounds anxious to find silence, and sleep. Since the incident at the gold dredge, they have been careful to lock the pickups whenever they had to leave them. But when they reach the trucks this night, after a fifteen minute trek, they find that a window has been broken and several sweaters stolen. Theft number two.

Overleaf: Descendants from
two enemy villages
join for the "payback"
celebration at Kindau.

The next day, at the village of Kolumba, the team comes upon another traditional ceremony that is an amalgam of old and new ways. In most Highland villages, when a young man seeks a wife, he sets in motion a tradition popularly called the "Bride Price," which is roughly the opposite of a Western dowry. It is expected that he will "buy" the girl he wants, as his forefathers have done for centuries. For the groom's family, the Bride Price is an opportunity to demonstrate wealth and prestige; for the family of the bride, a measure of recompense for their loss of a working woman. To establish goodwill between the two families, the groom's people offer somewhat more than they can afford, and the bride's people return half of what they receive.

The festivities are already in progress when the Cousteau team arrives. The groom's family, represented by his father, has completed financial dealings with the bride's family, whose spokesman is her uncle. The Bride's Price has been established as 6,000 kina and 4 pigs. With the delicate business taken care of, preparations have begun for a ceremonial transfer of the bride to the family of the groom, who, it turns out, is not allowed to be present as his future is being negotiated.

Wandering about, the team sees an odd intermingling of symbols: men chewing betel nuts but wearing baseball caps; a man wearing the traditional men's sarong, called a *laplap*, and a Bob Marley T-shirt; another man in a huge, crescent-shaped wig headdress, painted face, and sunglasses. Strangely, however, the impression is not that of old ways disappearing. It is as if the forms of behavior and ritual remain rigidly traditional, and the trappings of modern life merely represent new details.

Though they have adopted Western clothing, the villagers of Kolumba in the Highlands still follow ancient ways when it comes to marriage. Exchanging what is called the "Bride Price," the father of a young groom offers the bride's uncle 6,000 kina (about $6,000) and four pigs. Here, following tradition, the uncle returns half of the money. Accordingly, the bride is transferred to the family of the groom.

To symbolize the entry of the young woman into her husband's family, two relatives of the groom complete the Bride Price ceremony by parading about Kolumba with the bride on their shoulders.

A bracelet may be made of rubber bands today rather than bark, but it is worn in a traditional way. The materials change but not the structure. The new is integrated into the old.

As the bride is painted, sprinkled with Western baby powder, and adorned with some of the kina notes from her Bride Price, villagers arrange food into a buffet that strikes the Cousteau team as a kind of edible altar. Yams and bananas are piled high, sides of pork are laid out on banana leaves.

When the preparations are complete, the singing and dancing begin, the families assemble, and another seemingly endless series of speeches are offered by old men from each family. The ceremony is completed by a symbolic exchange of the bride. Two members of her family boost her to their shoulders and carry her around the area where the pigs and kina are on display, and when they finish, two members of the groom's family do the same. Finally, the Bride Price is officially transferred, the bride herself joins her new family, and the two clans join to feast for hours.

Sitting on the ground sharing the meal, the Cousteau team discusses the notion of a Bride Price. Martin Medan says the amount can vary from place to place in the country. As Anne-Marie finishes taking pictures and joins the team, Medan nods toward her. "How much would a woman like Anne-Marie cost in France?" he asks Blessington.

The diver ponders the question silently for a moment, then responds: "With or without the camera?"

Returning to their trucks, the Cousteau team finds that someone has again forced his way in, this time making off with Santee's expedition boots. Theft number three.

From the Mount Hagen area, the team follows the Highland Highway East to Mendi, which is generally thought of as the end of the road. Though the highway continues another fifty miles beyond Mendi, the road quickly deteriorates and traffic is scarce. The frontier character of the region may soon change, however, because new prospectors are combing the hills, not only for mineral wealth but for petroleum. Since twenty percent of Papua New Guinea's imports consist of oil and oil products, there is considerable incentive to find a domestic source of petroleum.

Cornu and Santee make contact with a local office of Chevron, which is exploring the region. If the company finds a significant oil deposit, they will construct a sixty-mile pipeline through the Leonard Murray Mountains to Kikori on the south coast, where the oil could be pumped to tankers.

At Cornu's request, the Chevron officials fly the cinematographer, Santee, Anne-Marie, and Gary Holland in a company helicopter to an exploratory well high up in the adjacent hills. The site, called Iagifu, is a leveled mountaintop, on which sit a drilling rig and scores of storage containers and dormitory trailers. Every piece of equipment there has been ferried to the site by helicopter. The four Cousteau team members spend half a day documenting the operation and interviewing its managers, then return to Mendi.

The team's ultimate plan is to reach Lake Kutubu, the country's second largest freshwater lake. From all accounts, the area and the four villages of Foi and Fasu people along its shores—numbering less than a thousand—remain little changed by the forces of development spreading through the Highland.

In part, this is because there are no roads to Lake Kutubu and no commercial flights either. To reach the lake as Highlanders do, one must walk over rough terrain for three days. The alternative is to arrange a charter flight to a village near Kutubu, so that the overland trek is reduced from three days to eight hours. Through their contacts with Chevron, however, Cornu and Santee manage to arrange for a free helicopter lift, and on March 28th, the team arrives at a place along the shore of Lake Kutubu called Taga Point, where they are welcomed at a small guest lodge.

After the exhausting drives, the frenzied work, and the confusingly mixed cultures of the last three weeks, the isolation of Lake Kutubu is a welcome refreshment. Cornu has been pushing relentlessly to film every story possible. He is exhausted, and the rest of the team is spent from the frenetic pace.

The lake, however, has a soothing effect. The surrounding valley is drenched in quiet, insulated by high mountains. The lake surface is a gleaming mirror, broken only by the occasional passage of a noiseless canoe. Across the water, the team sees a village called Wasaami built on an island in the middle of the lake: thatched huts, children frolicking in the water, men in canoes easily spearing fish, women gathering vegetables from luxurious gardens, sunshine, scenic forests, clean air, freshwater. A picture postcard of Paradise, says someone.

The team meets two women on their way to a marshy area where they will spend the day making *sago*, the most important traditional food of the Highlands. Cornu, Holland, and Anne-Marie tag along to document the process, which probably began with the first ancient settlers in Papua New Guinea, and has continued with little change in technique or tools through countless generations.

An exploratory oil well operated by Chevron stands at Iagifu near Lake Kutubu in the mountains above the Highland town of Mendi. The government of Papua New Guinea hopes to find substantial oil reserves in the Highlands, but exploration and recovery are difficult because of rugged terrain and local village land ownership.

Near Lake Kutubu, two women begin making *sago*, the most important food staple of the Highlands. A sago palm has been felled by men just before it is about to flower, when its starch content is highest; now village women wielding stone adzes dig out the exposed inner pith of the tree. (Domesticated pigs, like the one in the foreground, routinely wander freely about villages.)

Sago pulp is carried in sacks to a makeshift trough fashioned from the tree's bark, where the women will spend most of the day pounding it and soaking it in water.

Dark water in a bark catch basin covers the finished *sago* flour—a white starch paste produced by mashing the pulp and straining the juice through a fibrous mesh filter. The women will carry the starch paste back to the village, where it is packed into a hollow bamboo stalk and cooked over an open fire.

During the Cousteau team's stay of nearly a week, Anne-Marie rises early one morning for a swim in the lake. The sun has just risen, and the entire setting around the lake is one of unbroken quiet. In her diary that evening, she writes of the moment:

"A light fog was still hanging suspended above the water, and the lake was perfectly still. The colors of day had not fully emerged; everything seemed buried in half-tones, with an overlay of gray. I entered the water and found, to my delight, that it was warm and soothing.

"Somewhere far across the lake, a woman began to sing softly. The sound had an unreal quality, seeming close by and far away at once. Her lilting voice was lovely, and it echoed across the water. She played with this, singing a few words, listening for the echo, then singing again.

"Suddenly, somewhere behind me on my side of the lake, a man began to sing in response. The effect was mesmerizing and beautiful: two gentle voices drifting back and forth through the fog, a wall of mountains around me lit in the subdued colors of dawn, a crystal-clear lake below me as calming as a mother's womb. Floating dreamily, I could think only that I felt as if I were suddenly present at the first morning of the world."

On the last day of their stay at Lake Kutubu, the team spots a Chevron representative on his way to the island village of Wasaami, and they secure his permission to film. Peter Sandery, a former patrol officer, has been assigned the task of preparing villagers in the region for the possibility of future oil development. If a profitable deposit is discovered, it will be incumbent on Chevron to negotiate with local landowners for the rights to construct a pipeline to the sea.

In the men's house of Wasaami, Chief Tumbi Tagayu tells Sandery that his people welcome the coming of the oil company. They feel that the government of Papua New Guinea has long ignored their requests for a road linking them to Mendi and Mount Hagen, a development that could lead to a school at Lake Kutubu and the array of opportunities open to other villages along the Highland Highway. If petroleum is discovered around the lake, the oil company will build the road so long denied them by the government.

Life in the village of Wasaami, on an island in the middle of Lake Kutubu, remains largely unaffected by the outside influences sweeping through much of Papua New Guinea.

J.-M. C.: Later, pondering the future of this isolated mountain valley and lake, Jean-Paul recalls meeting Ben Joseph, the village leader negotiating with the gold mining company near Bulolo. Joseph had reached an awareness of the double-edged nature of development. He had mixed feelings, knowing that his people might stand to lose as much as they gained from the flood of money and material headed their way.

But here in Kutubu, Cornu realizes, the notion of development and progress is still a heady dream. For Chief Tumbi, it looms up as a distant golden cloud with no discernable dangers. This journey through the Highlands, Cornu later tells me, has taken our team through several stages of contact between the long-isolated villages and Western civilization, through cultures that blend the two worlds into an array of subtle distinctions, as varied as the countless shades of gray that can be mixed from pure white and pure black.

On April 3rd, Easter Sunday, a Chevron helicopter returns our team to Mendi. When they reach the site where their trucks are parked, only one of the vehicles remains, and it has been badly vandalized. It is the fourth theft, and whereas the other incidents involved minor losses, this time an entire pickup has been stolen.

The police are summoned, and the situation grows in complexity. It seems that the thieves who absconded with the pickup had just robbed a nearby business office. Don Santee's imagination flickers to a movielike chase scene in which an army of police is in pursuit of a white pickup with Cousteau Society logos emblazoned on the sides.

The logistical problem confronting Santee is a bleak one. Not only is the stolen truck unavailable for use, the Mendi police decide to impound the second pickup as evidence of the crime. Standing alongside a half ton of expedition cameras, sound gear, and baggage, the team is suddenly stranded. Santee tries to reach a car-rental agency to lease more vehicles, but everything is closed for Easter. There are no scheduled flights leaving Mendi. After several telephone calls, Santee finds a charter pilot. With all of the persuasive powers he can muster, Santee cajoles the reluctant pilot to forego his Easter celebration and fly the team to the coastal town of Wewak, where they can catch commercial flights back to Moresby or set out on the next leg of the trip into the Sepik River area.

Taking off, the plane circles over Mendi. The thin ribbon of the Highland Highway leads away in opposite directions, toward the beginning of our team's journey and a world deeply altered already by outsiders seeking riches, and toward the little-touched land to the west, only now awakening to change. Behind them is the fragile tranquility of Lake Kutubu, below, scattered villages where elders still recall the days of furious paybacks and young people dream of a future with automobiles and portable radios.

Some of these Highlanders are impatient to have the white man's "cargo" and have shifted from the unsuccessful "cargo cults" of their parents to direct procurement of goods left unattended.

Across these valleys below, the inevitable material civilization of the future approaches. Some villages are thoroughly transformed by it; some find ways to integrate its technological fruits into their ancient ways of life.

But everywhere, the invasion of the Highlands is not so much physical as it is spiritual. Once village warriors could drive away invaders with bows and arrows or fearful visages of mud and vegetable dyes. But neither mud nor bright feathers nor spears can frighten away the yearning invading the minds of their own youth, a yearning for the enchanting magic arriving from afar, a yearning for shiny wristwatches and fast vehicles and singing boxes.

Guided by a local villager, the Cousteau team inspects a sacred cave along Lake Kutubu where the remains of revered ancestors are kept. In white shirts from left: translator Martin Medan, Marc Blessington, and Expedition Leader Don Santee.

THE CENTER OF FIRE

My life's

amusements have

been just the same

Before and after

standing armies

came.

Alexander Pope

On the outskirts of Rabaul, two youngsters play among the rusting relics of Japanese armaments from World War II. Allied aerial raids on Rabaul represented some of the heaviest bombardments of the war in the Pacific. Half of the 300,000 Japanese stationed on New Britain died during four years of fighting.

In the summer of 1942, the factories and shipyards of Seattle, Washington, were frenetic with activity. The Japanese attack on Pearl Harbor six months earlier had triggered an industrial upheaval in America as assembly lines raced on overtime schedules to meet the demands for new military hardware. Seattle had become a leading production center in the scramble to outfit the Allied forces in Europe and the Pacific. The Boeing aircraft plant was supplying planes that would eventually play a key role in both theaters of the war, and Seattle shipyards were rushing out vessels to bolster Allied navies.

Several wood-hulled mine sweepers were under construction at a shipyard called Ballard Marine, among them a J—Class ship dubbed with the wartime designation "J—826." The vessel was finished in August, and dispatched to the British Navy under the Lend-Lease program for service in the Mediterranean. After the war, the minesweeper was sold to a ferryboat operator on the island of Malta, who gave it the name it would bear from that time on—*Calypso*. In 1950, the minesweeper-turned-ferryboat was acquired by a young French naval officer named Jacques-Yves Cousteau, who had recently developed a technique for exploring the undersea world and needed an expedition vessel. The ship was modified accordingly and sailed off into history.

While the minesweeper that would become *Calypso* was still on the shipyard blocks in Seattle, crews at the Boeing plant less than ten miles away were completing scores of large bombers whose austere nomenclature—B—17, B—25—would ultimately reverberate through accounts of the war's most dramatic engagements.

One of these aircraft, designated B—17 Number 4124521, left Seattle to join the war in the Pacific within days of *Calypso*'s departure for the war in Europe. The bomber was flown to Australia, where it became part of the U.S. Fifth Air Force. Called "Flying Fortresses" because they were among the largest aircraft built to that time, B—17s were invariably adorned by their crews with a painted nickname and symbol across the nose. Number 41—24521, because of its last two digits, was christened "Black Jack." From Australia, the plane was sent north to Port Moresby. Little more than a month old, *Black Jack* flew into a tumultuous air battle that would eventually be regarded as one of the critical turning points of the war.

When World War II broke out in the Pacific, Japanese and Allied strategists soon shifted their attention from the sensational opening rounds at Pearl Harbor and Midway in the Hawaiian chain to the constellation of islands sitting between Australia and the Asian mainland in the western South Pacific. Though geography was important, the compelling reality that would draw hundreds of thousands of combatants to these serene seas for some of the war's most violent fighting, and would determine the dominant force in the Pacific, involved resources. Indonesia (then called the Dutch East Indies) and Southeast Asia were rich in the raw materials needed to fuel military forces—tin, rubber, and, most important of all, oil. If petroleum-poor Japan controlled these oil fields, it would be a formidable military power. Without them, it was doomed to defeat.

Consequently, Japanese forces rapidly spread southward, quickly overrunning the major centers of Allied power in Hong Kong, the Philippines, and Singapore. By January of 1942, only a month after Pearl Harbor, they had reached the island of New Britain off New Guinea, which became their farthest outpost. From here, they would prepare an assault to conquer Australia.

If the Allies were to prevent a Japanese lockhold on the most important resources of the Pacific, they would have to halt them where they were, then try to turn them back island by island. Routed from the Philippines, American General Douglas MacArthur moved his headquarters to the Papua Hotel in Port Moresby, and the stage was set. Early in August, 1942, an Allied land force 600 miles east of Milne Bay began a bitter struggle for control of the capital of the Solomon Islands, Guadalcanal. And the same month, a titanic battle that would determine the course of the war and the destiny of millions of people erupted across the peaceful islands and seas of New Guinea.

The Japanese had established their headquarters in Rabaul, the capital of New Britain, and had scattered airfields across an arc of small islands off the north and northwest coasts of New Guinea. The Australians and Americans converged on Port Moresby, and built their first outlying airstrips in Milne Bay and on its offshore islands, including the Trobriands. From these bases, the two forces took to the air in a mutual attempt to annihilate one another in a relentless storm of bombing raids that continued for three years.

Shortly after midnight on July 11, 1943, *Black Jack* took off from Port Moresby on one of these raids. The assignment for the ten crew members aboard was to drop a load of demolition, fragmenting, and incendiary bombs on an airstrip near Rabaul. The 500-mile flight was uneventful, but as the B–17 neared the Japanese stronghold, two of its four engines began to fail. Both lost oil pressure and began to vibrate so violently that one had to be feathered, the other cut to half speed.

Though the plane lost altitude, the crew managed to reach Rabaul and release their bombs. But as they fought to keep the twenty-ton bomber airborne on the return trip, severe storms encircled. With only two functioning engines, the plane was unable to climb above the weather. The crew was forced to fly directly into the clouds where, because it was now impossible to keep a heading, they became hopelessly lost.

By the time *Black Jack* emerged from the storms, it was nearly out of fuel. The crew sighted a coastline, but they were unable to identify it. When it became obvious that they would have to ditch the plane, the men looked for a reef near shore, hoping to put the heavy bomber down softly in the shallows. At 7:20 A.M., nearly an hour after sending out a radio SOS, *Black Jack* skimmed across waters near Cape Vogel and came to rest about 100 yards offshore. The crew was alive, although three men in the rear of the plane had been badly injured when impact with the water ripped away the ball turret.

Unfortunately, they had missed the shallow reef. The B–17 stayed afloat about forty-five seconds, enabling the men to inflate a life raft and get out. Then it disappeared, plunging out of sight in 150 feet of water.

Ashore, in the village of Boga Boga, several people had seen the plane crash. They watched as men climbed from it into a rubber boat, struggling to help three men who were badly injured. When the tiny boat began to drift seaward, village men paddled out in their canoes and towed the crew to shore. Villagers rushed to comfort and feed the airmen, who tried, across a language barrier, to express their gratitude for the rescue. Eventually, an Australian float plane evacuated the three injured men, and the others were picked up by a motor launch.

J.-M. C.: In 1986, forty-three years after it set out for Rabaul loaded with bombs,
Black Jack was discovered accidentally by three divers on a Christmas holiday.
Through their efforts, the plane was identified. Though she had since been
visited by a few interested divers, the old B–17 remained undisturbed from her
final descent through a liquid sky to the sandy seafloor off Boga Boga.

When we learned of the B–17's existence, and saw the stunning photos of it
taken by David Doubilet, we determined to visit Black Jack during the Papua
New Guinea mission. I asked Falco to take Calypso to Cape Vogel during the
passage from the Louisiade Archipelago to the Trobriand Islands, and I ar-
ranged for Papagallo to fly me directly to the ship.

To rendezvous with Mike Sullivan and Papagallo, I flew from Port Moresby
to Alotau in a six-passenger Beechcraft operated by a national airline. As we
descended to the vacant-looking Alotau airport, I realized that I was looking
down upon a remnant of history. The landing field below me was built by the
Americans and Australians in the summer of 1942, and it was called simply
"Number One Strip." Constructed in only 22 days using steel matting, a tech-
nique that would be employed throughout the South Pacific as the war pro-
gressed, the airstrip at Alotau became a major staging center for thousands of
Allied aircraft.

Shortly after its completion, a Japanese amphibious landing force attempted
to overwhelm the base at Alotau and get a foothold on the New Guinea main-
land. Somehow they erred, coming ashore to the east of Alotau at the site of an
immense swamp. Nearly ten thousand Australian combat troops were waiting,
and a bitter battle ensued. Though the fighting continued for eleven days, the
Japanese never recovered from their initial landing mistake, and they with-
drew. It was the first defeat of Japanese land forces during the war.

Mike is waiting, and together we lug my accompanying bags of dive gear and
crew mail through the heat and humidity to Papagallo. With his red hand-
kerchief characteristically worn in a rolled sweatband around his head, Mike
could be mistaken for a Rock musician, but his steady judgment in the air, and
his careful maintenance of our float plane on the ground, have made him a
valued member of our team for more than ten years.

On this particular flight, as we travel backwards in time to visit a classic
aircraft in a famous theater of war, I know that Mike shares my exhilaration.
His love for flying, developed early, has lasted through a stint in Vietnam, and
through bush pilot jobs all over the world, from Africa and Alaska to Indo-
nesia. As we take off from Alotau, he asks if he can join the dive team on their
descent to the sunken B–17.

We climb quickly to slip through a mountain pass and sail northward for
Cape Vogel in a cloudless vault of blue. As we skirt the coast, I search the horizon
in every direction, imagining what it must have been like forty-five years ago,
when Japanese and American pilots looked for one another in these same skies,
nerves taut, peering down at these same vast expanses of blue, at the same
turquoise-rimmed islands and mottled green slopes. Through the glassy sea,
submerged fields of white sand appear from above as ghostly images hidden
in a blue darkness. Occasionally, I see rusting metal hulks tangled among
shoreline foliage, and I wonder if they might be the remains of Japanese landing
craft.

At last, the sight of white Calypso sitting at anchor before the village of Boga
Boga. We circle twice as Mike gauges the water surface. By radio, we learn that
the ship's film crew wants us to land near Calypso in order to capture a striking
shot. But Mike decides the surface is too rough near the ship. In the lee of a tiny
offshore island he sees the gentler waters he wants, and the film crew obligingly
jumps into Zodiacs to reframe their shot.

Near the village of Boga Boga at Cape Vogel in southeastern Papua New Guinea a crippled American B–17 crashlanded just offshore during World War II; local villagers helped rescue the ten-man crew. The plane—dubbed *Black Jack*—rests 150 feet below the surface just beyond the shallow reef at the right center of the photo.

Boga Boga villagers welcome *Calypso*'s team with a *singsing* dance and feast. Drums and dancing continued uninterrupted for four hours. Eventually, to the delight of villagers, several of the Cousteau team joined the line of dancers.

Aboard ship, Falco tells me that we are required to obtain permission to dive here from the people of Boga Boga, since the reefs are village territory. Also, no one can go ashore until the elders have officially welcomed us. It turns out that Calypso *has been sitting here for three days awaiting my arrival, and Bebert has postponed the ceremonies pending my presence.*

Since I cannot abide waiting another twenty hours before diving to the B–17, I ask Falco to seek a temporary "permit" from the village chief so that we can begin this afternoon. I have no doubts this will succeed (and it does) since I am sending our seaborne version of a chief and I expect the Big Man of Boga Boga will accede to a request from the Big Man of Calypso.

After the second lunch seating is completed, we gather at the dive station on the rear deck. Bertrand Sion marshals his forces together with his habitual scowl, breaking into a wide grin when I point this out. Though a large man, he leaps about with surprising agility, scaling the supports of the helicopter platform to reach dive equipment stored in out-of-the-way niches.

As I watch the usual complement of divers suit up—Sion, Prezelin, Davis, Rosset, Pascaud, Gourmelen, Dupisson, Noirot—I count the silver suits about me, so that later, along the bottom, I can be certain no one has wandered away. I count twelve, including Bebert and me. That is two too many. Looking from face to face among the group struggling into their suits, I see both Sullivan and Braunbeck. The two pilots have pleaded with Sion to outfit them for a trip down to the old plane. They are levelheaded men in most circumstances but wild-eyed romantics when it comes to visiting an authentic Flying Fortress at the very site where it came to rest after a bombing mission. It strikes me that the twelve of us will look like a school of bizarre silver creatures as we descend together amid lights, cameras, cables, and fountains of silver bubbles.

And that is, indeed, the case. Our outlandish little squadron drifts down through cool layers of water, invading with light and activity a watery chamber that has slumbered through time beneath a veil of blue fluid. The water is not as clear as Prezelin and Davis would like for filming, but the murkiness adds to the sense of mystery in our minds as we approach the bottom.

As the outline of **Black Jack** *emerges from the haze directly below us, I feel again an emotion experienced before as we came upon the remains of a Greek argosy in the Mediterranean or a clipper ship near Cape Horn. It is a mixture of exhilaration and melancholy. The privilege of witnessing and touching some fragment of the past is thrilling, but the lonely presence on the seafloor of a vessel that was fashioned for the world of sun and air above, that once contained human life, is chilling.*

Yet as we arrive along the bottom, these dark thoughts give way to surprise at the size and condition of the bomber. I swim along each wing, shocked to find that despite their total span of more than a hundred feet, and despite the weight of four engines and the ravaging affects of immersion in seawater for nearly half a century, neither wing is touching the bottom. They remain extended like the wings of a bird still ready to climb the skies again.

Peeking through the open hatches, we see silt-covered equipment—radios, fire extinguishers, belts of 50-caliber ammunition. Antoine Rosset waves to me, pointing to a small air cylinder he has carried along. When I nod, he removes the larger tanks from his back, begins to breathe from the handheld tank, and enters a hatch. Now streamlined, he can work his way forward into the cockpit where, with a roll of his eyes and a big grin, he takes the pilot's seat and gazes out, as if steering the Flying Fortress on a raid of the coral rocks twenty yards ahead.

Checking my watch, I realize that our allotted time at 150 feet is already up. Rosset emerges from the plane and we all rise slowly, stopping for fifteen minutes of decompression when we reach the extra air tanks Sion has suspended below **Calypso.**

Calypso's Dive Team explores *Black Jack*. The engine at left is one of two that failed, causing the ditching. The nose, outfitted with two machine guns, is the only badly damaged part of the B–17. Perhaps, as it sank, the plane struck a rock ledge or nose-dived into the bottom, causing the gaping hole that reminded divers of two jaws angrily contorted.

Hanging in midwater, I feel adrift in time. Above me, the hull of a former World War II mine sweeper is a dark silhouette framed by the shiny underside of the water surface. Though she has been a home to my family and our comrades for nearly forty years and has achieved renown as a symbol of knowledge and peace, our beloved Calypso *was actually created as an instrument of war. Had the world not been convulsed in violence, she never would have been built. What an immense irony, I think.*

Below, now but a dim corpse enshrouded in water, rests another instrument of war that, unlike Calypso, *never made it home. I marvel again at the coincidence that these two craft have come together again. Both were built within miles of each other; and though they left Seattle for opposite sides of the world, they left at nearly the same moment.* Black Jack *was not even a year old when events sent her to a watery tomb and four decades of oblivion. While the downed aircraft has been little more than a shelter for fish all these years, the mine-sweeper has traveled the world's oceans uncovering their secrets. One of those secrets was* Black Jack, *and today the wartime sister-craft from Seattle has arrived to pay a visit. Time and historical events have come full circle, and diverse paths have suddenly intersected again.*

As we climb onto Calypso's *deck, I notice the two pilots, Sullivan and Braunbeck, talking fervently as they remove their dive gear, arms flailing, words spilling from their mouths simultaneously. Perhaps, as a man of the sea, I saw below a memorable part of the ocean. But as men of the air, they saw part of the history of flight, a species of aircraft they had read about as boys, an heroic airplane still struggling to get home. I saw a seafloor wreck coated with ocean organisms. They saw a nightmare shared by all pilots, and for them our visit was an experience not of exploration but of kinship.*

About four in the afternoon, when the dive team has showered and dressed, most of the crew climb into Zodiacs and speed to the beach at Boga Boga. A special trellis of palm fronds has been erected in welcome. Before it stand a village elder in full regalia of feathers and adornments and face paint and a small woman who introduces herself as Selena. She has learned English at the nearby Anglican mission at Tarakwaruru, and she will serve as a translator during the evening.

Jean-Michel is greeted first, as *Calypso*'s most important Big Man, and the crew follows him through the trellis and into the village. Suddenly an old man rushes the group, pointing a spear and shouting threateningly, as if he is about to plant the weapon between someone's shoulder blades. Recalling similar greeters weeks before at Fergusson Island, the Cousteau team assumes this is all great fun. Standing in a circle about the visitors, the rest of the villagers are consumed in laughter.

For ten minutes, the energetic elder hops about, the center of entertainment. Then, from behind a bamboo pen comes a parade of men and women, all dressed in elaborate headdresses, shell necklaces dangling everywhere, palm leaves attached to their derrieres like rooster feathers (called *as gras* in Pidgin). The men leading the parade all pound on long, thin wooden drums, known in Pidgin as *kundus*. Gradually, the dancers lead the crew to an open, thatched shelter in the center of the village, freshly decorated with flowers. When someone notes the amount of work that has gone into this preparation, Selena says that the village only holds such celebrations three or four times a year.

The team is invited to sit beneath the shelter on wooden benches while the dancing continues for several minutes. Before them, a long table sits atop pandanus mats, holding an array of cooked dishes—yams, sago, bananas, pumpkin stew, taro, and fish boiled in coconut milk. Though the roof blocks out the blazing sun, the air beneath it is heavy and unfreshened by breezes. Watching the dancers, most of the crew pull out handkerchiefs to wipe their brows. Interestingly, someone points out, the dancers out in the direct sunlight are not perspiring.

When the dancing is finished, the chief is brought out to meet the team. Though thin and weak, the old man walks with a proud, erect bearing. He moves from visitor to visitor, saying "Welcome" and shaking their hands. Behind him in a long line come all of the dancers, about thirty people, and several young women, all of whom follow the chief's lead saying "Welcome" and shaking hands. Some of the young women carry flower leis, which they drape over the crew.

When the long reception line ends, a woman stands before the table of food and reads a handwritten speech. "Dear Friends from Overseas," she begins, and proceeds to say with considerable eloquence that it is because of this plane and the help their grandfathers offered the downed airmen so long ago that the Cousteau team is with them this evening. For that they are very grateful. The entire village welcomes them and wishes "good luck to our dear friends from overseas."

While most of the team is sampling the buffet, a young father approaches Jean-Michel. After a polite introduction, he announces that his wife has just given birth in a hut at the edge of the village. In honor of the visiting men and their ship, the couple has decided to name the baby boy "Calypso."

Jean-Michel is elated. The young man asks if he would like to see the infant. Of course, and immediately the entire team joins in a procession to his hut. The grandmother appears with the baby, who is still wet with amniotic fluid. Cameras click, the film team circles the gathering to document the moment. Selena makes a brief speech, saying that because of the new child's name, the villagers will remember *Calypso*'s visit every time they see him throughout his life.

Calypso remains at Boga Boga for two days so that Jean-Michel and the underwater film team can fully examine and document the B–17. While the divers are descending each morning and afternoon, the rest of the crew has time to carry out work that can be difficult while the ship is under way.

Dr. Raineix sets up a medical office in the *carré* between meals, treating a growing number of tropical ailments. Some are relatively minor problems: Braunbeck has been bitten by a centipede, several men are wrestling with the digestive maladies common to travelers, and all must be warned to follow the schedule for malaria pills. But other problems are more worrisome. Already he has forbidden diver-geologist Pierre Mollon to dive because of the severity of his ear infection, and since there seemed little prospect of improvement in the endless humidity, he has been sent home. Rosset has an open sore on his leg that seems to grow worse no matter what Dr. Raineix does. He is about to be pulled from the diving team, too. In the meantime, he has become the subject of a medical experiment.

Knowing that an increased supply of oxygen in the blood can sometimes speed up the healing process, Dr. Raineix has prescribed that Rosset spend an hour each day in the decompression chamber. While the young diver reads magazines, Sion increases the pressure, forcing more oxygen into his blood. Though it is too early to judge the effectiveness of the inventive treatment, it does not seem to be helping.

Completing the filming at Boga Boga, *Calypso* sets out on a northeasterly heading for Bougainville Island. Somewhere north of the Trobriands, she passes through an invisible demarcation, meaningless today but a frontier of violence between 1942 and 1945. The islands and the seas to the north were controlled by the Japanese. Most of the islands and seas to the south, by mid-1943, were in the hands of the Allies.

Aerial sorties raged back and forth. Gradually, the superior supply lines established by the Allies began to give them the upper hand, and the Japanese were forced to withdraw northward. At the beginning of hostilities, Japan held virtually the entire north coast of the mainland and most offshore islands. At the time of surrender in 1945, they controlled only the northern tip of New Britain, all of New Ireland, and a wedge of the north coast around Wewak.

The sudden flood of foreigners into a world little removed from the Stone Age, foreigners with awesome machines of violence, had a bewildering and profound effect on the people of Papua New Guinea. Before the war, there were about 5,000 Europeans and 2,000 Asians living in the country. Within months of Pearl Harbor, a steady stream of Japanese soldiers began to arrive, eventually totaling as many as 300,000—half of them destined to die here. The combined Allied force of Australians and Americans was nearly as large.

For many villagers, it was probably never clear why the hordes of strangers had invaded their world, or why they were trying to kill one another as they swept across it. And they surely never understood why they themselves were being directly and indirectly drawn into a conflict between foreigners. The effects began almost immediately. The ever present danger of aerial bombardments and military restrictions on sea travel limited local fishing and caused a temporary halt in the ancient Kula Ring. To assist the foreigners, some 55,000 nationals were conscripted into service as carriers, laborers, and guides (Australians dubbed their conscripts the "Fuzzy Wuzzy Angels"). Many of these conscripts suffered through extreme dangers in battle, as well as poor food and unsanitary conditions.

In the battle zones, village life was completely disrupted and bombings took a high toll. This was caused, in part, by the difficulty Australian and American airmen had in locating ground targets. Often the planes bombed and strafed innocent villages, destroying houses, gardens, and animals, and killing or wounding terrified villagers.

Yet, when the smoke of battle finally cleared, the war had left some gifts behind. Because islands were valuable mostly as air bases, both forces left in their wake usable airstrips that facilitated the development of national aviation after the war. Roads had been carved out by the occupying forces as well, leaving some islands as recipients of a free transportation network. The coral road used by the Cousteau team on Kiriwina Island is an example. Built by the Allies when the Trobriands were a strategic location, the road remains today the only automobile path from one end of the island to the other.

The war also changed forever the world view of countless people in Papua New Guinea. They saw wondrous inventions never dreamed of, learned about medicines, rode in powerful vessels and vehicles and airplanes. Some nationals, especially those conscripted, traveled widely within their own country for the first time, and the results were the emergence of a more unified cultural identity and the notion of political independence. On the outside, a whole generation of Japanese, Americans, and

Overleaf: Seen from *Calypso*'s helicopter, the beauty of the Jaba River floodplain on Bougainville Island belies the area's ecological problems. The river system is the principal receptacle for waste rock and tailings from the massive Panguna Copper Mine located in the distant mountains. With new mining operations gearing up in many parts of Papua New Guinea, the country's fragile tropical environment may face severe strains in the future.

Australians became aware of Papua New Guinea, and the Australians, moved by the help of villagers throughout the country, began to rethink their mandate, leading eventually to the nation's complete independence in 1975.

Yet for all the profound change that rocked parts of the country, especially the larger towns, remote regions quickly returned to the ways of their ancestors. An anthropologist visiting the Trobriands in 1971 was surprised to find the culture remarkably unchanged from accounts of the days before the war.

For many Trobrianders, it seemed, the war was looked upon mainly as a bothersome interruption in their Kula rituals.

On April 22nd, *Calypso* arrives along the coast of Bougainville. During a meeting of team leaders earlier at Boga Boga, it has been decided that the ship will spend a few days here to search for World War II wrecks and to investigate a massive copper mine on the island.

Prezelin, Zlotnicka, Rosset, and Pascaud rent a car and set out to investigate the mine. Braunbeck eventually joins them in *Felix*, so that Prezelin can film the site from the air.

A planning meeting in *Calypso*'s chart room: from the left are Chief Diver Bertrand Sion, Jean-Michel Cousteau, and ship's captain Albert Falco.

In many Highland villages, poinsettia bushes provide colorful natural fencing, often rising ten feet high. Their characteristic red bloom is not a flower petal but a leaf.

Arriving at the Panguna mine, named for the porphyry copper deposit it exploits, the team is astonished by the scope of the operation. Surrounded by dense rain forest and tropical stillness lies one of the world's largest man-made holes in the ground. When the ore is completely extracted, the pit will measure nearly 8,000 feet across and around 1,200 feet deep. It would take two Golden Gate Bridges to span the hole, and if the Empire State Building were set at the bottom, only the antenna on top would rise above the rim of the mine.

The Panguna copper deposit was discovered in 1964. Though it amounts to a vast treasury of copper, and smaller amounts of gold and silver as well, the ore is extremely low grade. The copper content of the rocks excavated is only one part in 200. Thus, to make the mine profitable, it must turn out a tremendous volume. That requires an operation using immense equipment and 4,000 people working in three eight-hour shifts seven days a week. The result is a production of some 130,000 tons a day for processing to copper concentrate. The bulk of this material is shipped to Japan, West Germany, and Spain.

When the Bougainville Copper Mine at Panguna started production in 1972, it trebled Papua New Guinea's annual volume of foreign sales. (Copper ore remains the nation's largest single export.) Though eighty percent of its profits go to public shareholders and Australian corporate owners, twenty percent remain with the government of Papua New Guinea. The government also receives taxes, and company policy mandates that nationals fill most of its jobs.

Beyond the scope of the mining operation, the Cousteau team is interested in its impact on the environment of Bougainville Island and its waters. During the construction phase, the sedimentation load of the adjacent Pinei River increased so dramatically that fish were eliminated from the waterway. Recognizing the disruption of local subsistence economies, the company compensated villages along the river with $20,000 a year for five years. When construction ended, the river gradually recovered, and its fish returned.

The greater problem is the daily accumulation of waste rock removed from the bottom of the pit and the tailings produced during treatment of the ore. Almost ninety-nine percent of the material originally mined has to be discarded, and there is little alternative but to dump it in a nearby valley. While the company has tried to find ways to secure the wastes and

Overleaf: The Panguna Copper Mine on Bougainville is one of the largest man-made holes in the world. The immense pit is excavated by four-story-high shovels that can scoop twenty-two tons of ore. The dump trucks at the bottom of the picture can haul one hundred and fifty tons of rock. Forty-five such behemoths roam the terraced roads.

keep them from eroding into freshwater streams and to use them somehow as new agricultural beds, nothing has yet succeeded completely. The
Jaba River system remains the principal receptacle of wastes, and the
company's future plans are to pipe the matter beyond the valley and into
the sea at the river delta. There is a monitoring program to determine
environmental impacts, but the massive dumping seems likely to continue
whatever the results of monitoring, since the only option seems to be
halting the mining operation.

During his reconnaissance trips in advance of the ship, Cousteau biologist Dick Murphy has visited Bougainville and learned of considerable
resentment toward the mine in sectors of the local community. Predicta-
bly, Murphy reports, people who have lost their traditional lands, even if
well-compensated with money, tend to feel cheated eventually as they
perceive that foreigners are getting wealthy on the resources that once
sustained them.

Presently, there is an effort under way to restore the ecology of the Jaba
River floodplain. Murphy puts the mine's supervisor of environmental
programs in touch with scientist Mark Brown, who has worked with The
Cousteau Society on environmental evaluations and is directing the re-
construction of an ecosystem damaged by extensive phosphate mining in
southern Florida. Since there is little information available on such resto-
ration programs, the mine operators welcome the help of Murphy and
Brown.

Before the Cousteau team leaves Bougainville, they sail *Calypso* past a
section of coastal waters deeply stained by the runoff from the mine. It
seems clear that the mine has a profound effect on the freshwater and
marine environment below it and that, while part of its profits are dis-
bursed to the country as a whole, its damages are borne entirely by local
people and the environment that has long sustained them.

On April 28th, *Calypso* enters the harbor of Rabaul, at the northern tip of
New Britain Island. The setting before them is stunning. The quiet, palm-
shaded town, with its dramatic backdrop of volcanic peaks, has been called

beautiful city in the South Pacific." Beguiled by Rabaul's
[...] t is possible to forget that it was once a center of fury during
[...] ar II and remains a volcanic catastrophe waiting to happen.
[...] e Cousteau team has learned, the ultimate source of Papua New
Guinea's luxurious natural habitats and lodes of copper, gold, and silver
riches is the uplift through time of minerals from deep within the earth.
Sitting atop the meeting point of three major plates in the earth's crust—
the Australian plate, the Pacific plate, and the Bismarck plate—the country and its islands have been periodically fertilized and enriched by pulses
of volcanic activity. The Bougainville copper deposit, the gold hidden in
the Highlands, and other mineral caches only now being discovered are
the results of this fiery elevation of materials through the volcanic arteries
of the earth's crust.

Rabaul is at the heart of these tectonic fulminations. The harbor itself is
the caldera of a volcano, which collapsed on one side about 1,400 years
ago and was flooded by the sea. The most seismically active part of Papua
New Guinea, Rabaul still registers slight earthquakes nearly every day,
and its surrounding peaks are reminders that the city has a questionable
future.

Six volcanic cones encircle Rabaul, formed around the rim of the
original caldera. Mount Vulcan, the youngest of these cones, appeared for
the first time as a low-lying island after an eruption in 1878. In 1937,
while some 500 Tolai people were holding a festival on the island, it
suddenly exploded, killing everyone and rising over a 27-hour period into
a 650-foot peak joined to the mainland. When Mount Vulcan had quieted,
after depositing yellow pumice, ash, and dust as a blanket across Rabaul,
Matupit—a second volcano across the harbor—came to life, erupting for
three days. Matupit last exploded in 1943, but it still emits sulphur vapors
to this day.

A *Calypso* diver examines
an unexploded bomb
stuck in the seafloor
alongside the sunken
Japanese freighter
Kanshin Maru near Rabaul.

A war memorial at
Wewak, near the
mouth of the Sepik
River, pays tribute to
the thousands of
Japanese originally
buried here in a mass
grave then exhumed
and returned to Japan.
Japanese troops held the
Sepik region during
most of World War II
but paid a heavy
price. Of 100,000
men stationed here, only
13,000 remained alive
when a formal
Japanese surrender
took place at Wewak
in September 1945.

In 1971, Rabaul was shaken by a tremendous earthquake and flooded by the resulting tidal wave. In 1984, a Stage II Volcanic Alert was declared, and the entire town of 15,000 people prepared themselves for a sudden evacuation. Some women and children were sent away, and aircraft were kept standing by for a massive airlift. Gradually, the threat dissipated, but the residents of Rabaul still live in full knowledge that their city, and their lives, could be extinguished suddenly.

Shortly after the disastrous eruptions of 1937, a volcanological service was established in Rabaul. Scientists there were able to give a six-month warning before the 1943 eruption of Matupit, and their continued vigilance imparts at least a partial sense of security among Rabaul residents. In 1985, the Volcanological Observatory found what appears to be a new volcano forming in the long-quiet caldera of the harbor.

During their stay in Rabaul, the *Calypso* team hopes to make some excursions in the Diving Saucer deep into the caldera of the harbor, in hopes of seeing some volcanic activity along the seafloor. While Thierry LeGuennec works to correct minor problems with the submersible, the team sets out to visit the sunken remains of World War II around Rabaul, an undersea cemetery of ships and planes that may be unparalleled anywhere.

When their planned island-by-island southward expansion was halted in the Solomon Sea, the Japanese were forced to alter their plans for Rabaul. When first taken in 1942, Rabaul was intended to be merely a

During a dive to a Japanese fighter plane near Rabaul, Cousteau pilot Michael Sullivan clowns for the camera. Without the knowledge of his diving buddies, Sullivan carried an old flying headset and scarf below, then climbed into the coral and sponge-encrusted cockpit, creating a startling image of "flying" through liquid winds, like a seabottom Red Baron.

Off New Hanover Island, a Cousteau diver lowers an air hose through the hatch of a World War II Japanese minisubmarine. The tiny hatch and cockpit forced the cameraman to squeeze into the sub without his scuba tanks. The small craft had sat upright and undisturbed in sixty feet of water for some forty years until discovered recently.

supply center for the forward march. Suddenly it loomed as their last outpost, and they took measures to make it a stronghold that could never be overtaken. They dug 300 miles of underground tunnels around the city, with enormous stores of armaments, as well as hospitals, bunkers, and barracks. Though Allied bombers—including *Black Jack*—would drop some 20,000 tons of bombs on Rabaul, turning it into a wasteland nearly as bleak as Hiroshima, the Japanese held on. They were still defending the city from their subterranean fortress when surrender came in 1945.

One result of the Allied bombing raids was the sinking of ships and planes, at least forty of which still litter the seafloor around Rabaul. On May 1st, the *Calypso* dive team makes their first dives to a haunting Japanese freighter called the *Kanshin Maru*. They survey a huge cavity surrounded by metal that seems rolled backward like the lid of a sardine can, apparently the spot where the lethal bomb entered the ship. They pass through the bridge, finding little of interest beneath a thick blanket of silt, then descend into a cabin on the lower deck, where their lights reveal a human skull.

During a meeting aboard ship, Murphy has warned the team to expect such remains in certain wrecks. Their presence is a chilling reminder of the countless human tragedies now largely lost to history.

Brazeau, Murphy and Shapiro, in fact, have been in touch with the U.S. CIL Search and Recovery Team in Hawaii, an American military unit set up after the Vietnam war. The team's popular name is "The Skull Team." When unaccounted-for planes or ships are discovered in remote parts of Southeast Asia or the Pacific, The Skull Team flys to the site and conducts an investigation to identify the craft and any human remains. Two or three times each year, they arrive in Papua New Guinea at notification by the government that an old wreck has been found in the sea or jungle. There are more World War II aircraft still missing in Papua New Guinea, The Skull Team tells Brazeau, than from any other place in the world.

Undersea remains can mean long periods of diving, but jungle-covered wrecks may be even more difficult to investigate. Often, The Skull Team descends by ropes from a hovering helicopter, then cuts a landing pad amid dense foliage so the aircraft can set down.

Such explorations can be dangerous, as the Cousteau divers realize during their probe of the *Kanshin Maru*. Through gaping holes in the ship they spot an undetonated bomb in the bow, and another in the stern. And lying on the seafloor alongside the wreck are more bombs and several torpedoes, none of which has yet exploded.

In succeeding days, the dive team visits several other wrecks: one ship spectacularly situated in a nearly vertical position; a freighter whose interior seems almost untouched, like an undersea residence complete with machine shop, bathrooms, kitchens; and several Japanese aircraft.

During one of their last evenings in Rabaul, Prezelin, Amaddio, Rosset, Le Meur, Dupisson, Jo Guillou, and Eric Dayou drive into the mountains behind Rabaul to a village of the Baining people. There they witness one of the most spectacular dances still performed in Papua New Guinea. As the team watches, children of the village build a large fire, playfully mocking the adult dancers to come by leaping about the edges of the flames.

When the fire has produced hot coals, the Baining Fire Dance begins. From behind village huts comes a parade of dancers in bizarre costumes. A sphere of leaves bulges about them, so dense that the only body parts visible are their legs. They wear large bark-cloth masks, many with haunting visages, to portray water and land animals—crocodiles, birds, butterflies, praying mantises.

The dancers move forward and backward at the fire's edge in grotesque motions suggesting the creatures they represent, briefly stepping onto the hot coals with bare feet. Gradually, they remain longer and longer on the coals until, just as the team has begun to wince in sympathy, they leap into the fire causing a burst of sparks, and the dance ends.

Driving back to *Calypso*, someone remarks on the symbolism, probably unintentional, of the Fire Dance. Across the ages, the people of New Britain have lived atop a volatile and fiery world. Their ancestral legends tell of moments when the earth beneath them exploded and burned, and their fathers remember the storms of fire that dropped upon them from man-made "skyboats." Today, the ground shakes each day, and there are fears of the great cataclysm still to come. How appropriate it seems that their most cherished dance should take place at the edge of a fire, involve extraordinary endurance of painful heat, and reveal in the vocabulary of human dance the possibilities of human courage.

A Fire Dancer in the village of Baining on New Britain Island leaps barefoot onto hot coals, performing a ritual known in his village since earliest times. Dance masks, representing island animals and taking several days to fabricate, must be discarded in the forest after a dance, never to be used again.

RIVER OF THE CROCODILE MEN

We are crocodile

and sago;

they are cassowary

and yam.

Manambu saying

Racing ahead in a Zodiac, Marc Blessington, left, and engineer Paul Martin lead *Alcyone* through floating vegetation on a Sepik tributary. The Papua New Guinea national flag flies amidships.

On April 29, 1988, a curious vessel enters the harbor of Madang, along the northern coast of Papua New Guinea. Local people on the docks are baffled by its appearance. It seems long and broad for a sailboat, if that is its nature, and too small to require such towering smokestacks, if it is a diesel ship. The driver of a tourist van from a Madang hotel thinks it is a submarine, although he has never seen a white submarine. A dockworker says it looks like an immense steam iron.

The mystery vessel is Cousteau's revolutionary windship *Alcyone*, arriving to join the expedition after a mission in the Bering Sea, followed by a stop in Tokyo to demonstrate its technological innovations to Japanese shipbuilders and a layover in Guam.

What appear to be smokestacks are, in fact, two hollow cylinders that act like vertical airplane wings. An aircraft is able to climb the skies because the profile of its wings produces a disparity in air pressure below and above them. Since the pressure below is greater, the wings are lifted upward on the passing airstream.

Alcyone's Turbosails use the same principle to produce forward motion. Wind streams more rapidly across one side of the Turbosails than the other; the resulting greater air pressure on one side creates the horizontal equivalent of "lift" and propels the vessel along the sea surface. Each cylinder sits atop a base that can be rotated for maximum exploitation of the wind, and a fan at the top of each cylinder draws passing air turbulence through perforated panels into the hollow interior and out the top, greatly reducing potential drag.

The invention does not vastly change the physics of sailing—canvas sails also take advantage of a difference in air pressure—but the Turbosail captures wind energy so effectively that it has proven five times more efficient than conventional sails.

The purpose is not to replace engine power but to supplement it. Depending on wind conditions, *Alcyone*'s Turbosails, operating simultaneously with her two diesel engines, can reduce the ship's consumption of fuel by as much as forty percent. With sufficient winds, of course, the engines can be shut down completely. Shipboard computers control and blend the two power systems for maximum fuel efficiency at a steady speed of 12 knots. In theory at least, the vessel's computer program is so elaborate it could handle the variables of weather and sea conditions and follow a precharted course across an ocean without a single crewman aboard.

J.-M. C.: My father and I decide that **Alcyone's** *first assignment during the coming weeks will be to carry out our exploration of the great Sepik River. Ironically, the decision has nothing to do with her Turbosail propulsion system, since the low, swampy plain we will enter is only lightly and occasionally swept by winds. But her draft of eight feet is slightly less than that of* **Calypso,** *making her more maneuverable in shallow regions of the river and its tributaries.*

In some ways, the Sepik is the Amazon of Papua New Guinea. Although the Fly River carries more water, flowing south from the Highlands, the vast catchment of the Sepik makes it the largest river system in the country. Beginning in the mountainous central spine of the island, it races down steep slopes, rushing in turns northward and westward, then dropping to meander eastward through a flat alluvial plain. Though the basin of jungles and swamps it crosses on its way to the sea is only 250 miles long, the Sepik flows in such dizzying twists and turns that it takes 700 miles to make the trip.

Like a liquid conveyor belt, the river has transferred vast loads of soil from the mountains to the plain, creating a mushy wetland floor that lies just a few feet above sea level. Though the shoulders of a few mountains rise here and there from the vast swamp, it is for the most part a fluid prairie of marshes, natural canals, and lakes.

The silt streaming out of the mountains often accumulates in the loops of the river, eventually blocking them and forcing the water into a new channel. As a result, the Sepik plain is littered with oxbow lakes severed from the main river. Many of the lakes are more abundant in fish, crocodiles, and water birds than the main river because silt has settled to the bottom, producing water of greater clarity.

Though most of the plain is thickly carpeted in long grass and the edges of the river are lined with wild sugarcane and reeds, occasional stands of rain forest crop up where the land is well drained. Most Sepik villages have been established in these miniature riverside jungles.

Whereas the Amazon is celebrated as a watery zoo teeming with piranhas, dolphins, manatees, and crocodiles, the Sepik is nearly barren by comparison. Only forty-three species of fish have been identified in the river, and the varieties most commonly eaten were introduced by scientists. The dominant animal of the river, the one creature of great mystery and respect, is the crocodile. It has been simultaneously hunted for food, worshiped as a powerful spirit, and feared as a demon for thousands of years.

But the spellbinding lure of the Sepik is not its nature but its humanity. Nearly 200 languages are spoken along its banks, making it the most diverse part of the most linguistically and culturally diverse country on earth. And nearly every one of its villages produces uniquely stylized artworks—spirit masks, shields, canoe prows, musical instruments, bowls, pots, and carved figures. In the Highlands, art is largely limited to the adornments and the enactments of dancing. But through the ages along the Sepik, virtually any man-made item has been fashioned as a piece of art, from spiritual house to household utensil. The Sepik region has been recognized by museums and collectors as the richest source of "primitive" art in the world, and the waterway has been called the river of art.

In part, this ancient and continuing integration of aesthetic vision into daily life may stem from the intense spiritualism of Sepik peoples. Though most cultures of Papua New Guinea regard the world around them as a domain of hidden spirits, villagers along the Sepik seem to go to more elaborate means to pay homage in art and ceremony to these native gods. Sepik spirit houses—each

Elaborate paintings of spirit faces adorn the gable of a *haus tambaran* in Maprik.

Carved animals along a *haus tambaran* roof in Maprik depict village spirits, sometimes representing the mythical origins of the peoples' ancestors.

village stores its art treasures in a sacred building, a haus tambaran *(tambaran is "spirit" in Pidgin)—are the largest and most elegant in the country. Sepik ceremonies seem richer and more complex than most. Rites of initiation, funerals, and various pageants portraying myths can last for days, involve enormous preparations, and, in some cases, inflict pain on the celebrants.*

We enter the Sepik, however, not as anthropologists or art historians. As explorers of the world's waters, our paramount goal is to learn how the planet's marine and freshwater habitats function and what part they play in local and global ecological webs. We are also trying to understand how humanity throughout the world exploits seas and rivers for survival, and how people treat the waters that sustain them—with respect, disinterest, or disdain. Sailing up the Sepik, we enter a realm where water is not merely valued as a source of life, but venerated as a source of divinity. In the view of many Sepik peoples, their sacred river still flows from the beginning of the world.

The general plan for *Alcyone*'s Sepik mission, conceived by Jean-Michel and the vessel's captain, Philippe Ruef, is to sail far up the river immediately, and to explore it leisurely during the return trip downriver. The Sepik team will be composed of sailing crew who have brought the windship south from Guam, and people transferred from other missions.

Arriving with Ruef are Chief Engineer Patrick Allioux, a member of the French Navy on temporary assignment to Fondation Cousteau, the nonprofit foundation based in Paris that is a sister organization to the American Cousteau Society. Also coming aboard are diver-navigator Thierry Stern; engineer Joe Cramer, who is completing a long stint aboard; and the vessel's French chef, Alain Furic. Engineer Paul Martin, a *Calypso* veteran whose Cousteau missions include the Amazon, arrives from the United States, enabling Cramer to leave for holiday.

With the completion of the Highlands mission, Land Team members Marc Blessington and Anne-Marie Cousteau are assigned to *Alcyone*. In recognition of his talents and dependability, Blessington is made Expedition Leader for the first time. From a Cousteau team filming humpback whales in Hawaii comes cinematographer Philippe Morice, replacing Cornu. Michel Verdier, the electronics and radio officer aboard *Calypso*, is transferred to *Alcyone* with the arrival of veteran radio officer Guy Jouas on the older ship. To complete the film team, sound engineer Mike Westgate, a free-lancer based in Aukland and a member of the recent Cousteau Society expedition in New Zealand, flies up to join the windship. Eventually, Australian Robbie Hunter, a contributor to *Calypso*'s recent film about the Great Barrier Reef, is also summoned to act as a second cameraman on *Alcyone*.

Before the ship can set to work on the Sepik, however, two Papua New Guinea nationals are welcomed to the team. To guide the ship in a river of considerable hazards—an ever-changing course that is not precisely charted, submerged logs, floating islands of vegetation—Ruef and Karen Brazeau have invited pilot James Kinjimali to journey with the ship. Born in a river village, Kinjimali has spent most of his adult life as a pilot and guide aboard the Sepik's only major tourist boat, the *Melanesian Explorer*.

The crew is completed with the arrival of Ivan Huasi. Though his presence aboard *Alcyone* is acceptable to all, it is in fact a requirement imposed on the team by the provincial Premier. Suspicions of the same sort confronted by Brazeau and Dick Murphy in the early stages of the expedition linger here. As East Sepik Province Cultural Officer, Huasi is along to act as a liaison with local villagers, but more importantly to observe and potentially to censor the Cousteau team's work.

Though the crew's projects and deportment are such that Huasi is never forced to exercise the power, it is within his authority to halt the filming and to confiscate the film at any time. (As a result of a bureaucratic misunderstanding, government officers attempted to confiscate film earlier from the Land Team, creating an awkward situation that lasted several hours before the error was uncovered.) It is another example of the wariness toward foreigners that, not without some justification, seems to permeate the nation's bureaucracies. In Huasi's case, however, the censor is soon just another crew member, helping with ship tasks and setting up stories that would be impossible to film otherwise.

The first week of sailing on the Sepik serves to introduce the team to the river's multiple delights, and to its one matchless vexation. From *Alcyone*'s deck, they gaze upon a passing tableau of enchanting beauty: exquisite sunsets casting the marsh grasses in red and orange hues as far as the eye can see, floating meadows that appear solid yet suddenly roll in the ship's wake, creating the impression of a rubbery world beyond the river's edge. In canals off the main river, still waters the color of tea mirror the billowing clouds scudding across the sky, turning them sepia.

Alcyone is greeted by local villagers as she approaches the Chambri Lake community of Aibom, a scene filmed from above by cameraman Philippe Morice.

There is an uncommon quiet across the landscape, reminding the team that life on much of the Sepik has not changed greatly since primordial times. From time to time, the ship passes a motorized canoe, but for the most part the only sounds beyond *Alcyone* are the rustling wings of water birds lurching into flight and the occasional bark of a village dog in the distance.

People seem to spend much of their life afloat. Dugout canoes are the taxis, trucks, and trains of river people. Long versions carry entire families or a shipment of handicrafts for barter with other villages. One-person models are used as runabouts by fishermen or shopping carts for women gathering village vegetables. Nearly always, the paddler is standing up straight, a skill common only among people who grow up on water. Children passing *Alcyone* are as adept as adults, and are said to learn to use a canoe about the time they learn to walk. For them, tiny dugouts serve the same function bicycles do for Western children.

But for all the fascinations of the Sepik, the Cousteau team finds itself under immediate siege from the river's ever-present, tormenting clouds of mosquitoes. It seems impossible there could be another place in the world so densely concentrated with the pests. Even crew members who have experienced the Amazon and the Alaskan summer are astonished at the volume and size of the Sepik's mosquitoes. Despite the scorching heat and humidity along the river, the team takes to wearing long pants, long-sleeved shirts, and high boots. There is a measure of comfort in this, but it seems largely psychological, since the insects are little discouraged and continue to bite through the clothing.

Though mosquito attacks are most savage during the morning and late afternoon, there is no unbreakable rule. Often, when the team is entering a village or swampy backwater, mosquitoes will suddenly appear even at midday and swarm over the crew. The odor of insect repellent becomes a pervasive part of life, along with continual swatting and scratching.

Villagers, while accustomed to the harassment, are no less vulnerable. Many carry small brooms made of marsh grass to flick about their bodies throughout the day. At night, they set firepots beneath the raised floors of their huts in hopes that the smoke rising through their sleeping chambers will repulse the insects through the night. They do this in part to protect themselves from the malaria carried by some mosquitoes. Though a greater health problem in some other regions of Papua New Guinea, it is nevertheless a widespread disease along the Sepik. Unfortunately, the precaution of filling their huts with smoke is nearly as hazardous as the malaria they fear, since respiratory diseases take a heavy toll throughout the villages, especially among infants and children.

On May 10th, *Alcyone* anchors in an inlet near the village of Kanganaman. The team has learned that a ceremony to be held this night in the village will involve sacred music. Hoping to make this their first glimpse into Sepik spiritualism, they set out by Zodiac to meet the elders of Kanganaman and secure permission to film the event.

Their first encounter is not with villagers but an aquatic plant called *Salvinia molesta*. The floating weed so clogs the edges of the river that the Zodiacs are nearly blocked from the village. For a quarter of an hour, the two launches surge forward a few yards, stop quickly to untangle their propellers, then progress a few more yards before the vegetation has again wrapped itself about the propellers. Anne-Marie, who had visited this same village a decade earlier, remembers it situated on the bank of a lake

Alcyone's Captain Philippe Ruef, left, and Sepik Expedition Leader Marc Blessington try to negotiate an infestation of the aquatic weed *Salvinia molesta*. Inadvertently introduced into the Sepik, the floating vegetation—native to the Amazon—spread rapidly without any natural enemies.

with little vegetation. From the research reports of Murphy and Shapiro, they recognize the *Salvinia* as an imported plant that spread like an infestation throughout the Sepik a few years ago. This is their first contact with it, and amid the curses it evokes this afternoon, they decide to study the effects of the plant as they travel the river.

A crowd waits on shore, and when the team at last breaks through the *Salvinia* and climbs from the Zodiacs, villagers lead them to a spirit house, a *haus tambaran*, where several men sit about smoking cigarettes wrapped in newsprint or carving methodically as they talk.

The spirit houses are an exclusively male sanctum in the cultures of Papua New Guinea. Even a young man cannot enter a *haus tambaran* generally until he has been through a rite of initiation in his teenage years. It is men who guard the village's sacred relics, who interpret events according to their knowledge of the local myths and legends, and who play the spiritual music.

Traditionally, women were never allowed to enter a *haus tambaran*, and though this ancient taboo has been broken occasionally in a few villages, it is still the equivalent of a felony in most. Women are not supposed to learn the secrets of the spirits, nor even to see the sacred bamboo flutes or the immense village drum called a *garamut*.

Thus, when Anne-Marie accompanies the rest of the Cousteau team to the entrance of the Kanganaman *haus tambaran*, there is a moment of tension. The elders see before them a woman, of course, but a woman with white skin who wears long pants, a man's expedition shirt, a photographer's vest loaded with gadgets, and a tangle of cameras and straps. Blessington asks if she can enter the house. There is some discussion, then the elders wave her in. It may be the first time a female has seen the interior of this spirit house.

When an agreement is reached with the elders, permitting the team to film their evening ceremonies for a fee, the crew returns to *Alcyone*. Two hours later, after dinner aboard the ship and the preparation of the camera and sound equipment, the team returns to the Kanganaman *haus tambaran*. Decorations of flowers and palm leaves now surround the entrance and hang about the interior. Morice, Blessington, and Verdier begin to set up floodlights.

Displeasure shows on the face of a Kanganaman elder, shown seated in the village *haus tambaran*, upon learning that the Cousteau team intends to film inside the sacred men's house.

The village men suddenly seem taciturn. Tension floods the *haus*. Vehement discussions break out among elders standing in huddles. Sensing that there is a misunderstanding, Blessington goes to the elders to inquire. They had not understood that the team meant to film their ceremonies. They cannot permit it. They have recently been deceived by a visiting writer, who broke his promises and published their secrets in a book. Now, women and children have access to information never divulged by all the generations of men who preceded them. They don't want this to happen again.

The first contact with Sepik spiritual practices has revealed that their orthodoxy is still vigorously followed, at least in Kanganaman. The Cousteau team packs their equipment, politely expresses their regrets for the apparent miscommunication, and begins to leave. An elder reminds them that the *haus* was decorated and, accordingly, the agreed upon fee still applies. Blessington pays, and the team returns to *Alcyone*.

The next day, the crew sails upriver to the village of Korogo, known along the Sepik for its voluminous production of artifacts. Once, village artists worked merely to venerate the spirits, but now their masks and carvings are in great demand among art dealers, who come to the Sepik from North America and Europe, and entrepreneurs, who sell them to tourists in Wewak and Port Moresby.

The team wanders through a lovely setting of grassy clearings where children play and through huts where women are preparing fresh fish caught in oxbow lakes near the village. Again, they find men carving in the *haus tambaran*. Drawing on the experience of the previous night, Blessington and Morice attempt to make their requests explicit. Could they film a village ceremony? The men of Korogo impose another ban on cameras. However, they are willing to play their flutes this evening if the team agrees to record only the sounds. No pictures, which could be seen by women.

At dusk, under a cloud of mosquitoes, the team returns. The *haus* is crowded with men and thick with smoke. A small fire provides flickering light, but its main purpose is to drive away the mosquitoes. The only other light source is a kerosene lamp. When Verdier has finished setting up his tape recorder and microphones, two men pull bamboo flutes from a frame suspended below the ceiling. For Sepik people, flutes have a transcendant holiness, since their lilting sounds are said to represent the voices of the ancestors.

That night, Anne-Marie describes the scene in her diary:

Carefully the men check the holes, blow lightly, and check again. The players face each other in the center of the house, barely visible in the warm light of the fire. The older of the two men leads. Like magic, the gentle sounds fill the room. The flutes seem to answer one another in short melodious waves. The atmosphere is heavy, humid, filled with mosquitoes. Everyone carries their own small broom and brushes himself regularly to get rid of the insects. Once in awhile, out of concern, somebody brushes me on the back. The local people and we, the foreigners, become one.

Closing my eyes, I let the melody talk to me. It is joy and sadness, cries and laughter, the fears of a child, the flight of a bird, wind through the trees, thunder on the river, the joy of a wedding, the despair of death, the loneliness of life, whispered secrets, love and hate. And my thoughts drift to the houses around us, where women and children are listening, too. Do they share or steal the magic?

Led by one of her Zodiac launches, *Alcyone* journeys up a Sepik tributary leading to Chambri Lake. The apparent riverbanks are actually floating meadows of aquatic grasses that may stretch for miles in either direction.

From Korogo, *Alcyone* sails through a shallow canal into a maze of connected waterways called Chambri Lake. The ship's guide, James, is originally from a Chambri village called Aibom, and he directs Ruef through the bewildering water network to his boyhood home.

The entire village pours out to watch the arrival of the strange ship. No vessel this large has come to Aibom in twenty-five years. Children climb onto tree branches hanging over the water or leap into canoes and paddle furiously toward *Alcyone*. Within minutes the deck of the windship is crowded with villagers. When James is recognized on the deck, smiles breakout everywhere. There are shouts and waves, and the pilot, who has not been here for three years, waves to the village like a returned hero. His mother, aunt, and a cousin clamber onto the ship, and when James introduces them to Anne-Marie, they break out in joyful dancing and singing.

James tells Ruef and Blessington the vessel can be anchored here, and the Zodiacs can be used for short trips to other Chambri villages. The first night at Aibom is marked by a powerful thunderstorm, and through the next day intermittent rain continues to fall. During a late morning break in the weather, *Papagallo* arrives from Wewak bringing soundman Mike Westgate and Mose Richards.

When pilot Sullivan has settled the float plane onto a narrow water channel near the ship, Zodiacs pick up the three men. As they climb onto the rear deck of *Alcyone*, after handshakes and hugs, the ship's crew warn the bare-legged, T-shirted arrivals to cover up their bare skin quickly. "Welcome to the land of the Mosquito," someone says.

After lunch, the team crosses the river in two Zodiacs to film the making of pottery, for which Aibom is renowned along the Sepik. A half-dozen women sit cross-legged in the shade of an open, thatched shelter, fashioning clay pots as large as amphorae and as small as drinking cups. Morice and Westgate are drenched in perspiration as they move rapidly to film the women and a conversation between Blessington and the headmaster of the Aibom school, who describes the process. While other villages specialize in wood carvings, spirit masks, baskets, and so on, Aibom has been the Sepik's chief supplier of pots for centuries. Blessed with a local source of fine clay, the village has used their products in barter with other villages, though now there is a tourist market for the pots.

A woman in the Sepik village of Aibom on Chambri Lake prepares flat pancakes made of sago. Her adornments are not ceremonial, merely her personalized workday makeup and hair ornamentation.

Aibom village has long specialized in the making of pottery. Women sculpt fine clay found nearby into pots that range in size from that of a demitasse cup to a huge stew kettle.

An Aibom woman returns home with a pot that went unsold during the day's market.

Sago storage pots are exhibited in the central commons of Aibom for inspection by a visiting buyer, who will sell the wares in Australia. Pots were traditionally a barter item for Aibom villagers, whose pottery is prized throughout the Sepik region.

Anchored off Aibom, the crew of *Alcyone* finds themselves unintentionally involved in a problem that graphically illustrates the continuing belief in spirits and the local reverence for crocodiles. After filming all afternoon in the village, the team returns to the ship for dinner. While the table in the *carré* is being set, Kinjimali appears with a fascinating piece of information.

It turns out that the villagers of Aibom are upset with the Cousteau team, because the site they have chosen for *Alcyone*'s anchorage is directly above the home of a river spirit, described as a powerful young crocodile. The storm of the previous night and the steady rains this day, they believe, are the result of the spirit's anger over the insult.

The team stands in the carré, looking at one another quizzically. Captain Ruef climbs to the rear deck and spots a lone man in a dugout canoe passing by.

"Is it true we cannot anchor here because there is a spirit?" he shouts.

The man nods.

"Where should we go?"

The answer is a shrug of the shoulders. Evidently, most any other place as long as it is devoid of spirits.

A worker in a crocodile farm in Angoram, near the mouth of the Sepik, skins animals that have reached commercial size. Though some crocodiles are raised here, most are purchased from villagers who catch them in the wild. The skins are sold to leather companies in Japan and Europe.

Left: Men from the Sepik village of Korogo, like other villagers along the river, hunt crocodiles for their skins and as food. The capture method is startling to outsiders: entering the murky river barefoot, hunters tread along the bottom until they step on a submerged crocodile then quickly dive to grab the creature about its jaws and pull it up. Though Sepik people generally worship crocodiles, they kill and consume them, believing the physical animals and the all-powerful crocodile spirits to be separate entities.

The prow of a dugout canoe on the Sepik River attests to the preeminence of the crocodile in the lore and spiritual pantheon of river peoples.

Ruef summons the team and they move the vessel downriver three hundred yards. Over a dinner of fish soup, beef Bourguignon, and éclair au café, the team considers the odd experience of displeasing a spirit, the first time it has happened to anyone's knowledge. The general conclusion is that no one will be surprised if the sky is clear the next morning.

After dinner, most of the team boards Zodiacs and motors to the village through the darkness. Stern and Ruef stand with flashlights directing thin beams of light on the water ahead, which is periodically illuminated by distant lightning flashes. Before they reach the bank, it is raining. The crew is drenched. "Perhaps the river spirit was angrier than we realized," says Blessington.

The people of Aibom are holding a singsing this evening, with full understanding that the team will be filming it. The team learns that this is not unusual, that tourists from the *Melanesian Explorer* are occasionally brought here in speedboats, and that a fee is paid for the performance. One aspect of the singsing will be different tonight, however. They have suggested, to the surprise of Kinjimali and the team, that village women will be admitted to the *haus tambaran* this evening at the end of the men's rituals. It is the first time this has been allowed.

The Cousteau team wrestles with an ethical problem. Their goal is to record life as it transpires normally in a village, neither directed by them nor altered to their specifications. Although the experiences of the last few days have seen resistance to the notion of filming sacred activities, in fact the problem elsewhere has been that many villagers seem too eager to please. If a cameraman asks, for example, whether men normally carve inside the *haus tambaran*, a "big man" will suddenly direct several men to begin carving inside the *haus tambaran*. It is not always clear whether this is the way of the village or an act to please the cameraman.

As it transpires, compared to singsings witnessed in Milne Bay by *Calypso*'s team, this one seems to lack a measure of energy and enthusiasm. The dancers are older, their movements, born of habit, seem mechanical, languid. At Boga Boga and at Iwa Island, both farther removed from contact with tourists, elders were joined in the dance troupes by young people. In both places, the local audiences were delighted by the performances, intrigued by the visitors. Here, the observers seem bemused.

About 11:00 P.M., the team returns to *Alcyone*, their foreheads still dripping with perspiration at this late hour, their brains still echoing the resounding throb of the *garamut*. The mood of the evening has left them tired, and somewhat depressed.

But the next morning, there is evidence that the villagers may have relaxed into a more traditional attitude when the cameras departed. Captain Ruef says that he heard the *garamut* still beating at 4:00 A.M.

Over lunch, Kinjimali talks of his youth in Aibom. In the 1960s and 1970s Chambri Lake was clear and beautiful, he says. There were water lilies, but no *Salvinia*. The team asks how a plant endemic to Amazonia came to the Sepik.

There are several variations on the story, Kinjimali says, and he isn't certain of the truth. One version is that a home aquarium filled with *Salvinia* was innocently dumped into the Sepik. A more elaborate story involves an Australian living in the Mount Hagen area, who imported some *Salvinia* for his private pond. A Sepik man in his employ noticed that the imported plant gradually eliminated unwanted local vegetation from the pond and decided it might be a good thing for a pond near his Sepik village. He carried *Salvinia* plants to the pond, where they flourished. During the rainy season, the area was flooded and the *Salvinia* washed into the Sepik.

However the Amazon weed arrived, it exploded like an unchecked virus, spreading rapidly through the main river, tributary streams, and linked canals and lakes. Channels were blocked; travel by canoe became arduous in most places, impossible in others. The proliferation was so widespread and dense that oxygen was depleted in the river, killing vast populations of fish. In villages dependent on fish for food, there was near starvation. Hundreds, perhaps thousands, of people were forced to leave the river and settle elsewhere.

For six years, Kinjimali tells the team, scientists searched for a remedy. Mass spraying of herbicides was considered, something that frightened most village leaders. Finally, the plant's natural enemy in Brazil was identified as a species of weevil. Shipments of these beetles were flown to the Sepik and released. But the scheme appeared doomed to failure initially. The Sepik *Salvinia* was not as nutritious as that growing in the Amazon, and the beetles were unable to reproduce.

Ironically, the only solution seemed to be a mass application of fertilizer to enrich the unwelcome plants. Fortunately, the experiment worked. The

A Korogo *singsing* dancer lights a leaf torch he will carry during the nightlong prelude to the scarification ceremony, traditionally carried out at dawn.

When the aquatic weed *Salvinia molesta* destroyed Sepik River fisheries in the early 1980s, many village men migrated to coastal towns, where they make a living by carving artifacts for tourists. This man left the Chambri Lake village of Wombun and now lives in a camp with fellow villagers near Wewak.

As the demand for Sepik primitive art has increased, the supply of local hardwoods has decreased alarmingly, forcing many carvers to use softwoods and imitate traditional spirit masks by staining the wood with dark pigments or charcoal.

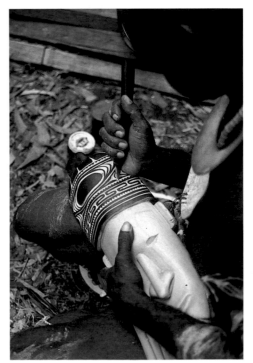

In a *haus tambaran*—"spirit house"—Sepik villagers store their treasured artwork and hold sacred ceremonies. This *haus tambaran* stands in the Chambri Lake village of Wombun.

weevils increased their numbers and spread wildly through the river. Less than five years later, the growth of *Salvinia* has been checked, permitting canoe travel through most parts of the river system, and new species of fish introduced into the waterways—such as tilapia and carp—have survived. Now, as the green monster recedes, some villagers wait to see if the alien weevil will turn out to be a problem. So far, the beetles seem content with the extraordinary feast of *Salvinia* before them.

The village of Wombun, only a half-hour's trip by Zodiac from Aibom, remains a victim of the *Salvinia* plague. Life in Wombun had long revolved around two sources of subsistence: the abundant supply of fish from Chambri Lake and trade in carved artifacts, for which the village was renowned. *Salvinia* eliminated the food source and made it nearly impossible to ship the artwork up and down the river by canoe. Nearly an entire generation of young village men left to establish a carving operation selling to tourists in Wewak. With the success of this satellite outlet, the migrants have not returned, leaving Wombun short of young men.

En route to *Alcyone*, Morice, Blessington, and Anne-Marie have visited the Wombun carvers in Wewak, filming their products and interviewing them about the great disruption of their lives. Now, with the ship anchored nearby, the film team spends an afternoon at Wombun documenting the other side of the migration story and interviewing elders who lament the transformation of their people into manufacturers of tourist mementos. While the masks, shields, flutes, sculptures and other goods sold at the Chambri camp in Wewak are well made, they have the patina of goods produced with tourists in mind, not ancestors or spirits.

As the *Salvinia* infestation has receded, fish have returned to the Sepik, some introduced by government fish-and-game managers. Near the Chambri Lake village of Kirimbit, a father and son retrieve a catch from a basket left for several hours along the river bottom.

The next morning, the camera team sets out by Zodiac for another Chambri village called Kirimbit. Blessington and Kinjimali have come here the day before and secured permission for the team to film local fishing techniques. The morning is cool and bright. The channel among floating weeds is as glassy as lacquer. The team looks across miles of floating vegetation that stretches in every direction. In the west they see distant hills that rise from the floodplain like overturned bowls, miniature Kilimanjaros surrounded by endless watery lawns. A glance backward at *Alcyone* evokes laughter. She appears to be sitting in the middle of a vast green prairie.

The fishermen of Kirimbit are waiting, and they set out immediately in dugouts. The floating caravan of canoes and Zodiacs passes along a narrow corridor of water through a dense mat of grasses, *Salvinia*, and water lilies. Three hundred yards offshore, where the water is about fifteen feet deep, the men stop at a bamboo pole driven into the bottom. A line made from a tough vine is attached to the pole, and now the men draw it in, retrieving a small palm-leaf basket. Inside there is a catfish which, seeking shelter along the bottom, has settled in the trap. The men smile, hold the basket and fish up for inspection, and identify the fish in Pidgin as a *bikmaus*. It is tossed into the bottom of a canoe and the party paddles on another two hundred yards to more bamboo poles. Stretched between them is a fishing net that reveals three snagged tilapia.

During the last afternoon at Chambri Lake, the film team stops at another lakeside village called Indingai. The men of Indingai are presently making a canoe behind the village houses, and Morice is eager to film the process. As an immense log is being hollowed out, Blessington interviews the village chief, Patrick Kandau, who describes the trees traditionally used for canoes, carvings, housing materials.

The villagers are faced with an enormous problem, Kandau says. The most valued hardwood trees are declining under the increasing pressure for production of carvings. The populations in Sepik villages are expanding, and there is no way to make money other than carving. Blessington asks why they need the cash produced by selling tourist artifacts. The chief mentions the need to pay for their children's education, the increasing costs of tinned food, which gained a foothold in the village as *Salvinia* destroyed their fisheries, and, among other things, the tremendous inflation in bride

Sepik men have devised innovative fishing techniques, which vary from village to village. This fish trap is constructed of thorn-covered branches shaped into a cone. Bait is fastened inside the cone and the basket is lowered on a line to hang just above the bottom. When a fish seeks the bait, it becomes inextricably caught on the thorns.

Though Western jeans and steel axes have become commonplace in some Sepik societies, the dugout canoe remains the principal means of river transportation. Trekking through dense rain forest near the village of Korogo, the Cousteau team encountered this young man practicing a craft learned at his father's side.

prices. Once, a young man could secure a wife with pigs and other local gifts. Now, even here in this remote village off the main Sepik, brides can cost 2,000 or 3,000 kina (roughly $2,000 or $3,000). The team marvels at the amount, wondering how villagers could ever accumulate such sums, especially if they are limited to the profits from artifacts, which routinely sell for 10 or 20 kina. Kandau says that the bride prices here are nothing. He has heard that prices in Port Moresby can reach 30,000 kina.

When the filming is complete, and the team is packing their gear, a sudden squall arrives. The villagers lead them to an open shelter. A young man named Daniel strikes up a conversation with Richards, then invites him to visit his hut. Inside, he walks about pointing out his belongings: four Aibom pots used as fireplaces for cooking and discouraging mosquitoes, baskets filled with sago hanging from carved hooks. On one wall there is a montage of photos clipped from magazines. Most of the pictures feature models in bathing suits.

Daniel says that a bamboo and palm house usually lasts about twenty years, then it must be reroofed and rewalled or even rebuilt if the framing is rotten. The corner posts and frame are hardwood, covered with a grid of bamboo, over which sticks are tied vertically to form walls. Thatched palm leaves are fastened across the top to form a roof. The spongy floor, suspended six feet above the ground, is made of flat slats.

The single great room is dark, and despite the smoky firepots, mosquitoes flit about. But, in midday at least, the space is comfortable, cooled and freshened by breezes penetrating the porous walls. Moreover, like the open spaces around village buildings, the interior is kept meticulously neat.

Opposite: As time allows, the village men of Korogo work to complete a new *haus tambaran*. The weathered and ornately carved corner posts of the new structure bear witness to both the esthetic impulses of Sepik craftsmen and the constant ravages of the tropical environment.

An orator's stool sits in the center of the *haus tambaran.* The mustachelike adornments on the spirit face are pig tusks.

The ornately carved roof post of a *haus tambaran* shows how Sepik peoples turn even the most prosaic articles of daily life into spiritual artwork. Tools, weapons, hooks for storing bags of food above ground, stools, tables, bowls, dishes, musical instruments—all are fashioned with divine or supernatural imagery.

151

Daniel speaks English fluently, the result of a year spent working for a construction company in Port Moresby. He saved his money and returned to Kirimbit to buy a bride. Several others in the village have done the same. The solution to the mystery of where young village men acquire their bride prices seems evident. They leave the village to work in a commercial center in order to accumulate enough money to acquire the woman they want, then return to settle in their native village.

On May 20th, *Alcyone* leaves Chambri Lake and sails back upriver to Korogo. During the ship's earlier visit to the village, there was talk of an extraordinary event to take place through the night of the 20th and into the morning of the 21st. The nature of the ritual intrigues the team, and they gain permission to return and to film it.

When a young man of Korogo is ready to pass from childhood to manhood, from the care of his mother to the society of men, he undergoes a dramatic skin-cutting ceremony, in which most of his body is covered in wounds that will resemble, on healing, the scales of a crocodile.

A Korogo man fashions a leaf headdress for an impending scarification ceremony, in which three young village men will be elaborately scarred in patterns meant to resemble the scales of crocodiles.

The Cousteau team has been granted permission to witness the ceremony, but they are warned that there are certain moments so sacred they cannot be filmed. To ensure against unwanted observers, a fence of palm and banana leaves thirty feet high has been erected around the *haus tambaran*. An all-night singing will be held in the *haus*, culminating at dawn with the scarification ceremony.

During the afternoon, the team visits with the three young men who will undergo the rites of passage. There is a notable sense of anticipation in their homes, where they rest with relatives and mentally prepare for the intense pain to come. The team is told that the initiates will be given a traditional drink this evening and betel nuts to help them endure the suffering. One young man declares his pride in being chosen by the Council of the Ancients for this honor and declares his lack of fear.

About 4:00 P.M. the dancing begins. Fifteen men form a sinuous line representing a huge crocodile and circle around the *haus* chanting and waving grass pompoms. After five circuits, they stop to rest. The same dance, however, will continue all night long, broken only by brief intermissions to smoke or chew betel nuts. Despite the solemnity of the occasion, the dancer acting as the crocodile's tail is the Sepik equivalent of a circus clown, whose elaborate gestures and comic antics make the women scream with laughter and the children hide.

Through the night the village remains a droning, noisy hive of activity. The drums pound endlessly, the dancers circle, the mosquito fires fill the air with the dull odor of smoke, women chatter, babies cry, silhouettes drift here and there through the red light of the flames.

At 5:00 A.M., as gray light begins to bathe the village, the team is led to another part of the village, where the three young initiates, heads now shaved, are surrounded by their male relatives and friends. When the time has come for the last circuit of the exhausted dancers, each of the initiates and male family members join the crocodile's tail.

Reaching the *haus tambaran*, the line divides. The dancers pass through the main door of the *haus*, but the initiates and their supporters must tear their way through a smaller, blocked door. Inside, the initiates must leap over a fire, then run through a gauntlet of men armed with sticks. While the initiates rush forward, a family "protector" tries to shield each from the blows of the men with sticks.

Now, the time has come for the scarification. Since first light, the village has been filled with haunting music: first flutes, then the slow, monotonous beating of a *garamut*, then the music of the thin drums called *kundus*, which are played at the edge of a stream near the *haus tambaran*, dipped in and out of the water to create a deep, cavernal sound. When Anne-Marie raises her camera to photograph the drummers, she is pulled back immediately. "You are not allowed," someone says. "*Tambu!*" (Taboo.)

In an open space alongside the *haus*, the skin-cutting ceremony begins. Later, Anne-Marie describes it in her diary:

One of the young men is now naked and sitting atop a canoe that has been turned upside down. His head and shoulders lie against his protector's chest. He chews on a stick that is said to be an analgesic and will help to control his screams. One or two men will do the cutting with a razor blade. This is the "modern way." A sharpened bamboo stick was used in former times.

I cannot see the first cut. A man steps in front of me intentionally. We are forbidden to photograph the cutting at all, which is sacred, although we are allowed to watch. I can see the face of the young man. He is in pain. Tears escape his eyes, and his teeth crack the stick as his head jerks against his protector's chest in a violent reflex. The protector's hand moves compassionately to the initiate's forehead. I am struck by the extremes in attitude, of inflicting pain and, at the same time, showing compassion, a gesture of tenderness among men.

Two men do the cutting, one on either side of the initiate. Another wipes the blood away with pieces of cloth rinsed in a bucket of water. They cut without interruption for about an hour-and-a-half: the entire chest, the arms, the back all the way down to the legs, almost to the knees. The cuts are between one inch and one-and-a-half inches long. The pattern is beautiful. Each village has its own.

When the young man is "finished," he must be totally cleansed. He can hardly stand. His legs and all of his muscles are shaking. As I look at him, totally exhausted, trying to stand properly, his body still folded, his back cut with hundreds of perfectly symmetrical red lines beautifully curved, I think of an accordion of cut paper being unfolded. I find myself in deep respect for the courage of the young initiate and the artistry of the skin cutters.

Young men start dancing. Outside the fence, the crowd waits attentively. Two of the mothers stand nearby. One wears a black net on her head and face. Now, carried on their protectors' shoulders, the initiates are brought out and shown to the village, then taken three times around a tree with a huge crocodile skull at its base. Then they are carried back into the *haus* to rest. They will stay there for weeks—healing, but also learning the traditions, the stories, the secrets of playing the sacred instruments, and the rules of the village.

It is time for everyone to rest. We, too, are exhausted. As we return to *Alcyone*, I still feel the tears and the pride of the mothers left outside while their sons were suffering.

A young initiate endures the long series of razor cuts that will leave him permanently scarred. The rite of passage will seal his membership in a select council of men who lead the village of Korogo, pass on its mythic tales, and guard its secret rituals and sacred artifacts.

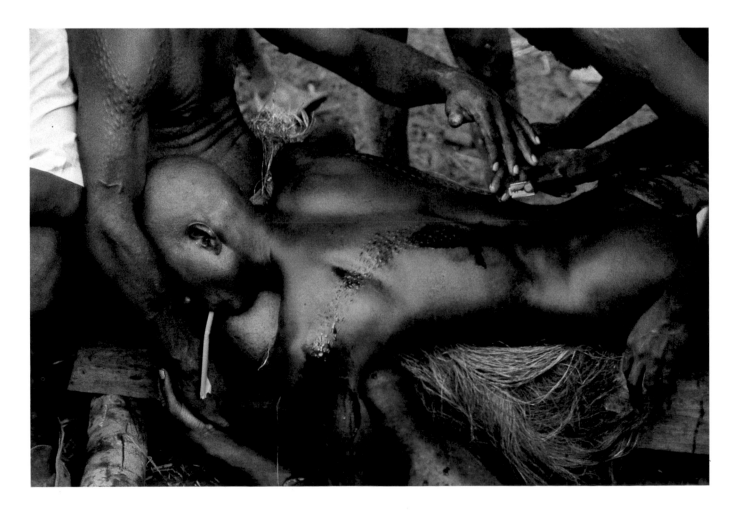

Too weak to stand, the initiate sits atop an overturned canoe and leans against a comforting relative. Tigasso tree oil is rubbed on his cuts to begin the healing process. Though the painful rite is now finished, the young man's indoctrination in village traditions and stories is just beginning.

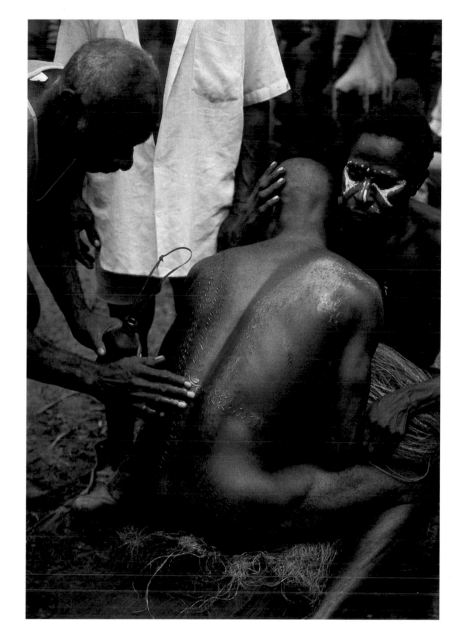

Along most of the Sepik, no spirit is mightier than the crocodile. Most villages hold the belief that their people are descended from ancient animals, plants, or natural forces, and most weave into their artwork heraldic emblems of their spiritual ancestors. But the great primeval crocodile is to most Sepik people the originator of the earth itself, fashioned from formless water, and the maker of the sky above, drawn out of the earth, and the creator of human beings to dwell among these great gifts. When foreigners first came in contact with men whose bodies were covered in scars, village elders told them these men had been swallowed as youths by crocodiles and had been reborn as "crocodile men."

Life changes along the Sepik, and life does not change at all.

RENDEZVOUS IN A BLUE LAGOON

Never imagine

that life at sea

is easy.

Jacques-Yves Cousteau

While one Cousteau Film Team records from the surface and another from the air, *Calypso* and *Alcyone* rendezvous near the Hermit Islands in the Bismarck Sea. The two ships had followed separate routes since their last meeting three years earlier in New York. *Calypso*'s itinerary had included the Caribbean, the Marquesas, Tahiti, New Zealand, and Australia; the windship had visited Cape Horn, Mexico, California, British Columbia, Alaska, and Japan.

J.-M. C.: *As the float plane races to leave the runway and loft itself into the sky above Madang, my mind wanders backward in time through a jumble of place names. Today, Mike Sullivan, Mose Richards, and I are on our way to join* Calypso *at tiny Garove Island in the Bismarck Sea. How many other times, and in how many other places, have I flown off to join* Calypso *in my life?*

As schoolchildren, my brother Philippe and I flew from the south of France each year to meet the ship in exotic locales and to spend our summer vacations as part of a crew unlocking the secrets of the undersea world for the first time. Algiers. Tunis. Nicosia. Port Sudan. Later, as a young man helping to handle logistics for my father, I set off to rendezvous with the ship in Madagascar, Fort-de-France, Kodiak, Callao. Through the past decade, leading expedition teams of my own, I have returned to Calypso *in ice-choked seas near Newfoundland, on the coffee-colored Rio Negro in Amazonia, along the refinery-lined lower Mississippi, above the coral reefs of Haiti.*

Emotionally, a journey to Calypso *is a return home. My mother lives there most of the time, much of my father's work is carried out there. Men who served as "uncles" to Philippe and me, such as Albert Falco, still manage the affairs of my floating family home. Perhaps it is like a farm boy returning to his family's homestead, where the fences and fields are familiar and beloved farmhands still carry out the daily tasks of planting and harvesting.*

This flight is a poignant one because my purpose is to sit with my father and plan a rendezvous between elderly Calypso *and her spry younger sister* Alcyone. *Over the past three years, since the windship pulled into New York harbor with* Calypso *at her side, successfully completing a transatlantic maiden voyage, the two vessels and their crews have followed routes half a world apart.* Alcyone *has rounded Cape Horn, explored the Sea of Cortez and the Channel Islands off southern California, and endured the cold seas of British Columbia and Alaska. To a great extent, these have been missions under my direction, and my wife Anne-Marie and I have frequently settled into the windship like a second home.* Calypso, *meanwhile, has undertaken missions in the Caribbean, the Marquesas Islands, New Zealand, Tahiti, and Australia, following routes and missions conceived by my father.*

Now, as we motor in Papagallo *through the warm tropical air of Papua New Guinea and my mind wanders from past to future, I realize that the coming rendezvous of our two ships will also represent a huge reunion of two generations—of sailing technologies, of crew members, and of family.*

We arrive over Garove Island about 1:00 P.M. From above, it looks like a green bracelet woven of foliage, floating on a cobalt-blue sea. Within the nearly complete circle of the island sits white Calypso, *three Zodiacs shooting from her flanks to prepare for our landing, looking like random missiles trailing white tails behind. As Mike banks around the interior of the island, I realize that it is the crater of a volcano, which has been flooded by the ocean from one side to form a perfectly sheltered and spectacular natural harbor in the middle of the Bismarck Sea.*

We circle until the film teams are in position and follow their request to land between Calypso *and a mission church that sits on a bluff above the water.*

My father greets us as we climb onto the stern, but soon retires to his cabin to recover from a stomach ailment in hopes of diving with his teams tomorrow. The crew mail is distributed, greetings and inquiries about families and children are exchanged, then Sullivan, Richards, and I sit down to a late lunch. The crew's eager questions force me to continue talking through the meal, bringing them up to date on activities aboard Alcyone, *in our Cousteau Society offices, and on Hawaii, where a team is filming the underwater drama of the erupting Kilauea volcano.*

With all flags flying and all support craft racing about in celebration, the two vessels sail toward anchorage in the pristine lagoon of the Hermit Islands, where the crews will join to explore unfamiliar reefs.

In *Calypso*'s chart room, Captain Jacques-Yves Cousteau and Jean-Michel Cousteau plan the final weeks of the Papua New Guinea expedition.

After lunch, we sail out of the bay to a spot about a mile off the southwest end of the island. Two red buoys mark the spot where the team has found a pinnacle rising to within thirty feet of the surface. On previous dives here, they have watched excitedly as barracudas and schools of tuna and jacks passed by.

We climb into diving gear and quickly slip down to explore the pinnacle again. Unfortunately, the water this day is disappointingly murky, so that our cameras will not capture the beauty of the reef and fish below. Yet gliding about I can see visual treasures. A winged pipefish the size and shape of a cigar hovers above encrusting organisms on a rock. With patches of pink, white, and yellow along its body, the motionless creature is camouflaged to near perfection. A school of silver jacks angles past us, quickly emerging from and disappearing into the fog of particulate matter surrounding us.

We peer down into crevices looking for reef creatures. A white-spotted puffer fish wanders by, passing through a group of black-edged damsel fish, its tail waving rapidly yet providing little forward motion, its single, white bottom tooth sticking out as if the creature were proud to display the tool used to pry shells from the bottom.

Opposite: Like all of its species, this puffer fish employs two highly effective defense weapons. It can quickly inflate to alarm enemies or make itself too large to swallow. As a further defense, its tissues contain a chemical that would poison a predator.

Despite its fierce countenance, the surgeon fish feeds on algae. Its popular name comes from a razorlike bone adaptation projecting from the base of its tail (not visible in the photo). When attacked, the surgeon fish can whip its body about in defense, wounding with its sharp blade.

Left: Colonial sea squirts, members of the subphylum tunicates in the *Chordata* phylum, are among the most colorful of reef creatures. Despite their apparent similarity to corals or sponges, sea squirts have a primitive nerve chord and gill slits, making them more closely related to vertebrates.

Below: A juvenile spider crab crosses the rippling surface of a coral, perhaps foraging by night for small bottom organisms or organic debris.

Right: The sacklike body of a sea squirt enables the creature to draw water in, capturing plankton and organic matter as they pass across gills within the animal.

Another example of the exquisite beauty of soft corals. Unlike reef-building corals, most of these colonial animals do not incorporate one-celled algae into their tissues. The tiny yellow spots in the tentacles are actually batteries of nematocysts, or stinging cells.

Looking like glass vases along the seafloor, tunicates filter water through their transparent bodies to extract food. Some tunicates incorporate distasteful chemicals in their tissues, which discourage potential predators.

With its elegant rose-colored polyps extended to feed in the dark, this colonial creature is just one of a bewildering variety of soft corals found on the reefs of Papua New Guinea.

Right: Along the bottom near Garove Island in the Bismarck Sea, branched arms reach out in all directions to capture plankton passing by in the currents. The feathery creatures in the center of the photo are crinoids. Gorgonian stalks can be seen at the top and a soft coral at the bottom left.

Above: Resting on a black coral, the tiny reef fish revealed by camera lights during a night dive would be difficult for predators to see on an otherwise darkened reef.

Below: Amid reef fishes, the gelatinous body of a soft coral extends into the plankton-rich currents, enabling countless polyps along the limbs to feed.

Above: With their budlike jaws, butterfly fish can feed by plucking invertebrates from the crevices of a reef. Evolution has provided this fish with a striped color pattern that swirls right through its eyes, making it difficult for predators to determine which is the forward end of the fish and thus which way it will dart when alarmed.

*The next morning at 8:30 A.M. we again dive to the pinnacle, remaining for an
hour, and a second dive lasting about forty-five minutes is made after lunch.
Neither dive is very successful. The water is again murkier than we hoped, and
our team of eight divers outfitted with lights, disgorging bubbles, and tended on
the surface by three Zodiacs proves to be intimidating to any fish schools that
might be in the area.*

*Just before noon, Falco, my father, and I stand before a navigation chart on
the bridge. It is time to create a plan for both ships during the coming ten days.
The diving at Garove is too poor for the intended filming, and there is a strong
current. My father wants to go elsewhere. Perhaps to Cape Matanalem at the
west end of New Hanover Island, where the divers filmed a giant jewfish.
Perhaps to the Hermit Islands, where Dick Murphy and I encountered some of
the richest reefs in our memory during dives more than a decade ago.*

My father meticulously measures off six hours of Calypso's *travel time on the
nautical chart using a compass adjusted to the width of a degree of latitude. He
experiments. Cape Matanalem to Manus Island, two twists of the compass.
Twelve hours. On to the Hermit Islands. Another twist. Eighteen hours. It could
be possible during the coming few days. Perhaps a night sail this evening to
Cape Matanalem, two days of diving, then on to Manus where the helicopter
could be dispatched for an aerial shot needed by the camera team, then on to
the Hermits without stopping. I could join* Alcyone *for a few days on the Sepil
and bring her to the Hermit Islands, where the rendezvous could take place.*

*The matter is discussed further in the afternoon, after the second dive of the
day, and made official with a telex to* Alcyone *and to Karen Brazeau in Moresby. Our "family reunion" will take place in the pristine remoteness of the Hermit
Islands. Since we have reached the decision late in the day, after I have made
two dives, one below a hundred feet, it is impossible for me to fly to* Alcyone *until
the next morning.*

*It is one of the odd aspects of the diver's life. Just as it would be dangerous for
me to descend again this day, according to the dive tables that limit our
exposure to water pressure, it could also be dangerous to undergo another
pressure change by rising into the sky two or three thousand feet. I must remain
at sea level for the night.*

At dawn, the ship arrives off Cape Matanalem, the westernmost point of
New Hanover Island. Two hours later, Sullivan sets *Papagallo* down on the
sea, and Jean-Michel is transferred to the plane by Zodiac. When the float
plane has disappeared in the southern sky, the dive team suits up, ready to
continue filming the huge jewfish, called *La Loche* in French, which has
been encountered earlier along the same reef.

Prezelin finds and films the fish on the first dive of the morning, and
Davis captures more footage of the giant on a second dive. Returning to
the deck, each describes a school of barracuda, which travels back and
forth along a ledge about one hundred feet deep.

May 24th is a raw, rainy day. Prezelin and Davis each leads a morning
dive. The jewfish is not around, but they find two green moray eels for
camera subjects.

At lunch, Captain Cousteau recalls a story from the experimental trans-
Atlantic voyage of the first windship, *Moulin-a-Vent*, a catamaran outfitted with a Turbosail, the precursor to *Alcyone*. He and radio officer Jouas
were sitting in the main salon one afternoon, somewhere in the middle of
the Atlantic, when the satellite communications system suddenly and

inexplicably began to send out an SOS alarm. They hurriedly squelched the message, but not before it was received by the Comsat station in Goonhilly, England. The call came in: "Are you in distress?" "No," answered Jouas. Then: "Please give us the name and license number of your radio officer." Cousteau took the microphone, thought for a moment, and responded.

"This is the captain of the vessel, Jacques Cousteau. I am deeply disturbed by this occurrence, and I have appointed a committee to investigate it thoroughly. We will report to you as soon as their report is tendered."

They never heard from the Comsat station again.

After lunch, and a general siesta for one hour, Prezelin and his team descend again. While they work seventy-five yards from the port side of *Calypso*, Captain Cousteau appears at the stern in his diving suit. Donning tanks and mask, he climbs down the dive ladder alone, shunning any help or companionship. He is determined to test his ears again. As three crewmen watch and Maupiti hovers with a mask and snorkel at the water's surface as a lookout, Cousteau swims down to 100 feet. After ten minutes, he returns, smiling. "Finally, these ears work," he says. "I'm ready for the next dive."

Since the diving is not very productive, Cousteau and Falco decide to get an early start on the eighteen-hour journey to the Hermit Islands. At 3:30 P.M., when the dive team has resurfaced and the Zodiacs have been raised to the rear deck by the crane, Falco enters the bridge. Sion, Sarano, and Dayou move to the bow to man the anchor windlass as it is hoisted. Falco gives the signal and the anchor chain begins to roll across the wheel of the windlass.

It stops abruptly, sending a shudder through the ship.

Sion, the chief diver, is sent below to investigate. Maupiti floats at the surface to keep a masked eye on the diver and relay any messages to the deck. Sion finds that the anchor has dropped through a narrow crevice between coral boulders. The combination of strong current and rolling seas stirred by an approaching storm has neatly wedged the anchor and chain into a twisted lockhold among the serpentine crevices of the reef.

It is now 4:30 P.M. To escape the reef before nightfall, Falco directs that a steel bar be sent down to Sion. Though reluctant to damage living coral, the captain knows that he has no alternative but to try to break off pieces of the reef in order to liberate the anchor.

When Sion surfaces again, unsuccessful, Falco slips into his wet suit and dives to have a look for himself and to work the steel bar. Another hour has passed, leaving about forty-five minutes of daylight. The ship's captain remains along the bottom for half an hour, then returns. "It is no use," he reports. "We will remain here for the night and work in the morning when more divers are available." He shakes his head in frustration but quickly smiles, as if to say, "So be it." Captain Cousteau, standing quietly, turns to a new member of the crew and says, "Never imagine that life at sea is easy."

The next morning, at first light, the divers descend to chip away coral rocks around the anchor using a hammer and cold chisel. They succeed, after alternating work teams for two hours, in freeing *Calypso* from its bondage to the reef of *La Loche*.

Some will recall the incident, but for most of the sailors it will likely fade away as just another problem in a life aboard ships. The only important deadline faced by a seagoing captain is the final morning of the voyage, whenever it comes, and the principal charge for that morning is that the ship be afloat and the crew alive.

By 8:00 A.M., *Calypso* is bulling forward at full speed westward toward Manus Island. For those not at the engines or wheel or on watch or repairing equipment, it is a day for washing clothes, writing letters, reading a novel, or sleeping.

The mood changes perceptibly, as if life aboard moved from a minor to a major key, to something rich and promising. The blood of sailors quickens underway; when their entire universe of bunks and gear and galley and friends are all headed toward something new beyond the horizon, slashing forward through water and air with the racy concept trembling through the vessel that excitement lies ahead, something unexpected or lovely or thrilling. People relax. People are more comfortable. The heat blows away with the constant breeze. Dreaded tasks such as painting the hull can be forgotten as the ship churns and the decks surge up and down. Captain Cousteau is wearing his red watch cap, Simone is laughing girlishly. "I love it when we're sailing," she says.

There is time to dream in a bunk, to ponder the mysteries of life while watching the radar and the autopilot console on the bridge. Heading 275 degrees. Position fixed at 2 degrees 22 minutes South, 149 degrees 30 minutes East. Speed 10.5 knots. Not an island, reef, shoal, breaker, or vessel in sight. Thunderheads arrayed about in the distance, with their carbon gray rain skirts, like singsing dancers beyond hearing. But straight above, a South Seas blue sky bluer than all connotations of the word blue mixed in the mind, all shades of blue distilled into the pure hue, into blue blue.

In his high armchair before the windshields on the bridge, Cousteau is feeling expansive. The subject of writing has come up. He cannot understand how one could turn from pen and paper to a word processor. All the sensual pleasure of writing would disappear, he thinks. He himself follows a ritual that is joyful and productive. He rises at 5:00 A.M. when he must write. He has a cup of tea, toast and marmalade, then moves directly to his desk (most commonly the round dining table in his Paris flat). He sits before a blank sheet of paper and agonizes over the first sentence. When at last it comes, he pens it carefully in his meticulous longhand, then admires it proudly, and then speeds ahead with the rest of the piece, which is now clearly evident from the bursting meaning that flows from the first sentence. Sentence after sentence seem practically to write themselves across the page. With each finished paragraph, he pauses to admire again. How fulfilling it is to have created another fine paragraph using his mind and his hand.

It cannot be the same, he thinks, clack-clacking away on a computer, seeing an electronic ant track accumulating. And besides, he raises his arms for emphasis, how can you *frame* the original draft manuscript of a great writer who worked on a computer diskette. He himself has collected a few precious pages of original manuscripts, with the handwritten notes and corrections in the margins etched in ink by the great novelists, poets. That is something. That has a value. It is history. How in the world, he raises his arms again, can you frame a diskette?

From the act itself, devalued by computer technology, in his strong opinion, he turns to the hardware. The computer is a wonderful tool, but it is dwarfed by the marvelous and befuddling capacities of the human brain. The "cells" of a computer can only offer a yes or no, a zero or a one. But the cells of the brain function with chemicals and electrical impulses that enrich their capacity, make possible endless shades and mixtures. Each cell is practically a computer itself.

Cousteau recalls a series of experiments conducted by some visiting scientists at the Oceanographic Museum of Monaco, of which he was a director for thirty-one years. They were interested in the intelligence of cephalopods, including squids and octopuses, and the Museum staff helped by collecting the animals. Cousteau himself has always felt that the octopus, armed with deft manipulative devices, good eyesight, and a significant brain, represents the highest order of the invertebrates. The creature, he says, does not have a substantial number of brain cells compared to higher animals, but it seems to get a lot from them.

So the visiting scientists took samples of brain tissue, examined them under the microscope, attached electrodes, and so on. They found, to their great surprise, that a single brain cell seemed to "talk" chemically and electrically to other cells. What is more, the surrounding cells appeared to "listen." When one cell stopped "talking," other cells seemed to "respond."

"There was a dialogue going on among individual cells!" he says, rolling his eyes, throwing his hands in the air again.

"Imagine the subtleties of communication and data retention available to a single brain cell with its chemistry and electricity!" he says. "Imagine the possibilities! And we have thirty billion brain cells in our heads!"

He laughs. "Imagine!" he says one more time.

Imagine is a word Cousteau uses often. It is a clue to his perspective on the world. Within the realm of the provable universe and observable physical laws, within the reasoning faculties of his beloved human brain cells, Cousteau imagines all of the possibilities. He invents scenarios, dreams up gadgets, constructs futures in his mind, and, perhaps most of all, plays with ideas as if they were toy trains and he were still a child genius.

Which he is.

The day wears on with no pause in the hum of the engines, the roll and pitch of floors and walls and bunks. Lunch seems more lighthearted than usual. At four o'clock, Braunbeck starts a cassette of his favorite movie among those in *Calypso*'s video library: *Rustler's Rhapsody.*

Midway, the pilot is called to the bridge, where Prezelin is trying to figure out if it would be possible to fly to Manus Island in *Felix*, film some abandoned landing barges from the air, and return before dusk. Braunbeck thinks it is possible, and the two men take off.

When the movie is finished, some of the team wander to the foredeck to watch for the return of the helicopter. They lean against the rail, staring ahead into a distant storm backlit by a sunset that is the color of glowing embers. A warm breeze licks their faces. The panorama is magical. The ship moves below them with the irregular motions of a living thing, not simply up and down as it slices the waves but up to the right, then up to the left, like an athlete whose shoulders roll gracefully in the dance of his sport.

A speck grows, the helicopter with its red light on, sailing directly out of the sunset toward *Calypso*, landing on the platform in dusky blue light. Falco and Cousteau grin, relieved. Prezelin describes how the shot they sought was too dark, then, in a moment of odd chance, just as they were about to leave, the sun emerged from clouds, bathing the scene below in gold light. "The shot was extraordinary," says the chief cameraman. Braunbeck shakes his head, chuckling. As he walks away, muttering to himself and anyone within earshot, he says, "Typical Cousteau luck."

After twenty-seven hours of steady sailing, *Calypso* approaches a narrow channel that offers entry to the eastern flank of Hermit Islands atoll. On either side of the vessel, flying fish begin to erupt from the water. Davis, Noirot, and Sarano grab their cameras to record the gliding flights. A fish takes off, leaving a wake the width of its fin-wings for ten yards, then rides the breeze as long as five, even ten seconds, before dipping back into the sea. During one take, Davis records a seabird diving to pinch a flying fish in its beak before it can escape.

As *Calypso* is carefully steered into the atoll entrance, the entire crew empties onto the foredeck. Staring over the side they marvel at the clarity of the water. It is as if they are peering down through a glass-bottomed boat. A spotted ray moves along the bottom, and a large grouper, easily visible. Corals and sponges can be made out from the bow, and the observation chamber seems to fly through an aquamarine sky, so crystalline is the water.

As if on cue, a pod of dolphins appears, leaping from the surface at the atoll's edge, approaching *Calypso*. Cousteau strides to the bow and watches with a grin that approaches a smirk, as if this were the expected welcoming party in Paradise. Through the clear water, the lithe creatures seem particularly graceful, playful. It is another moment set apart from the routine. Prezelin and Braunbeck, who have just risen again in the helicopter, hover off the bow to record a fairy tale scene of the white-haired seapriest and his young crew gazing at the flashing bodies of dolphins at the edge of a blue lagoon in the fabled South Seas.

Falco and Cousteau decide to spend the day exploring the coast of the atoll, searching for a pristine dive site. The Zodiacs are fueled, and the crews set out. The first dive is disappointing. As the divers descend along a reef wall, they swim into a strong vertical current that carries them down to 120 feet. The dive is terminated, and the ship moves to another location. The second dive is more successful: a school of barracuda is sighted, a jewfish, shoals of colorful reef fish. A buoy is attached to a coral head to mark the spot for future dives, and two more take place during the afternoon.

At 8:15 P.M., Cousteau leaves the crew as they finish a meal in the *carré* and climbs to the radio room. As agreed in advance, he will place a call through the Comsat phone to Jean-Michel aboard *Alcyone*. The satellite communications system is as convenient as any home telephone, but at $10 a minute, it is employed sparingly. Jean-Michel reports that they are a day ahead of schedule in their Sepik River exploration. The windship is already leaving the Sepik. They will stop in Madang, then head north to meet *Calypso* in the Hermits. So, almost three years exactly since their last joint sail, the wooden converted minesweeper and her high-tech, aluminum sister ship will tie up together along the edge of an atoll in the Bismarck Sea.

Dolphins frolic before a Cousteau Zodiac near the entrance to the Hermit Islands lagoon. Anne-Marie Cousteau makes photographs from the launch while Marc Blessington drives.

Opposite: Cousteau cinematographer Louis Prezelin, who directed much of the film work aboard *Calypso* in Papua New Guinea, and Bob Braunbeck, the ship's veteran pilot, descend to the helicopter pad as crewmen scurry to prepare the chocks that secure the craft.

Though on different vessels, Captain Cousteau and Jean-Michel Cousteau communicated daily to decide the course of the Papua New Guinea expedition, using ship's telephones, as well as telex and fax machines. As their two vessels pull alongside one another at the Hermit Islands, the process continues through walkie-talkies.

An hour before sunrise on the 27th, Falco orders *Calypso*'s anchor hoisted. The ship sets out on a westward course to intercept *Alcyone* along the west coast of the Hermits atoll. At first light, Braunbeck and Prezelin take off in the helicopter. Directed by radio from *Alcyone*, they find the windship twenty miles away, then follow it from above until, about 6:30 A.M., the two vessels are within sight of one another.

The setting could not be more dramatic: distant storm clouds lit with the golden shades of sunrise, two white ships steaming toward one another before an outcropping of South Pacific palm-lined islands, helicopter circling like a seabird, crewmen in Zodiacs speeding at the flanks of their respective ships. As the two floating stars pass port side to port side, people wave at each other, laugh, point, snap photos that will one day enter dozens of family photo albums.

Calypso and *Alcyone* circle slowly as the film cameras hum, Prezelin in the air, Davis on the deck of *Calypso*, Australian cameraman Robbie Hunter dashing from one shooting angle to another in a Zodiac on the surface. Anne-Marie Cousteau, in a Zodiac, and Didier Noirot, on *Calypso*'s foredeck, are steadily clicking still photos that will ultimately appear in books, in newspaper and magazine articles in many countries, and, blown up and framed, will hang on Cousteau Society office walls in New York, Paris, Los Angeles, and Norfolk.

Calypso follows a narrow channel into the Hermit Islands lagoon with the smaller sailing vessel following. By radio, tongue in cheek, Captain Cousteau tells his son that dolphins will arrive to welcome the two ships in ten minutes.

His estimate is off by twenty minutes.

Only one Cousteau craft is absent, and that is soon rectified. Soon after the dolphins have disappeared, Sullivan, in *Papagallo*, buzzes the two ships, flying only sixty feet above the water.

When *Calypso* anchors, *Alcyone* pulls along her port side and the crews tie them together. The helicopter descends to its platform. The seaplane is moored to the stern of the windship. In the mixing of teams from both vessels, there are handshakes among old comrades, and there are introductions of first-timers. For many of *Calypso*'s team, who have joined the ship within the last three years, it is the first opportunity to inspect the odd new wind-powered vessel.

Crew members with like positions gather in knots: divers with divers, engineers with engineers, film crews with film crews. Captain Ruef visits Captain Falco. Captain Falco visits Captain Ruef. Cousteau father and son clap hands and head for the bridge. Anne-Marie embraces her mother-in-law. The two Cousteau women have not seen one another for a year and a half.

A gangplank is laid across the gap between the two vessels and Simone, carrying her dog Yuki, boards the windship. The dog races about sniffing unknown legs, aluminum rails, peering down into deck ports and hatches. Suddenly he leaps up onto the gangplank and races, despite Simone's protestations, for *Calypso* and the comfort of familiar decks and legs.

At Jean-Michel's direction, a wind-surfing board stored along *Alcyone*'s deck is laid across two rails amidships. All hands are summoned to the deck of the windship, where paper cups have been set out on the surfboard table. To shouts and whistles, a six-liter magnum of champagne is carried from the bridge and handed to Maupiti. Captain Cousteau and Jean-Michel direct the Tahitian sailor to pop the cork and fill the forty-odd cups.

J.-M. C.: We spend our second day together in dives using men and equipment from both ships, and in planning sessions to organize the coming month.

In two separate dive teams, we make a total of four descents along the outside drop-off of the reef encircling the Hermit Islands. Water clarity varies, and there are occasional encounters with fish schools, but most of the concentration is on close-up photography of luxurious corals and creatures like the tridacna *clam. Wedged among the corals and sponges along the bottom, the giant* tri-dacna *appears from above as a stiff mouth with brilliantly colored, mottled*

Camouflaged to resemble a part of the reef, a grouper waits motionlessly beneath a branching coral. When a smaller fish or crustacean wanders too close, the grouper will lunge forward to engulf the prey in its powerful jaws.

One of the most common inhabitants of Papua New Guinea's reefs, and one of the loveliest, a Zebra surgeon fish warily eyes a Cousteau cameraman.

lips. Tiny round light sensors line each lip. Each clam sports an individual color and design. Some are a dazzling blue or green, some an earthy ocher or beige. "Psychedelic," laughs Davis at the end of a dive.

Tridacnas are the clams once portrayed in early underwater films as deadly traps for divers. When an unsuspecting hardhat diver stepped between its shells, the giant mollusk would clamp together around the victim's foot, fastening him to the bottom in a death hold. It made for stirring drama, but it was complete nonsense. No such treachery by the gentle bottom-dweller has ever been reported.

Along the shallow ridge of the atoll, color and light produce exquisite images. Among the clumps of corals and sponges are a few colonies of blue coral, which rise from the sand like bushy antlers the color of a pale sky. Surgeonfish graze on an algae with heartlike fronds strung together like necklaces. Brilliant green trumpetfish lurk in crevices, eyeing us warily.

Leaving the sun-dappled shallows, we cross deeper water within the lagoon to reach the ship, passing through spears of sunlight that pierce the fluid about us and play about the ocher hull of Calypso.

On a crowded reef, life quickly fills any open space. Here, a soft coral colony has attached to the empty shell of a dead giant *Tridacna* clam.

Two Cousteau generations explore the seafloor near the Hermit Islands: Jean-Michel in the Dive Team's new silver suits, Captain Cousteau in his preferred black suit.

Champagne at breakfast time gives the long-awaited rendezvous an air both festive and French. The meeting brought together old friends and introduced new crew members who had joined one of the teams since the last rendezvous three years earlier. From left: engineer and diving saucer pilot Thierry LeGuennec, marine biologist François Sarano, Jean-Michel, Captain Cousteau, deckhand and diver Teriihaunui ("Maupiti") Loyat and ship's captain Albert Falco.

On Sunday, May 29th, our last day together, Davis, Westgate, Hunter, Anne-Marie, and Phil McCombs, a visiting journalist, take a Zodiac to visit the village in the atoll, and to document the fishing techniques of Hermit Islanders. The filming takes the entire morning, since the villagers must move from one location to another in order to find fish. Their method is to create a circular wall of palm-leaf nets, trapping fish within, then spearing them from above.

Meanwhile, I lead morning and afternoon dives from the deck of Calypso. All in all, we are overjoyed with our choice of the Hermits for the rendezvous. My worries that the waters here would no longer be as pristine and rich as I recalled have proved groundless. And other variables that could have spoiled the reunion have in fact blessed it: the weather has been perfect, the sunrise that illuminated the actual moments of our meeting at sea was soft and golden, the dives and the camaraderie have been marvelous.

Yet one thing has not really come to pass as I had hoped. Though my father and I were able to spend some time along the bottom during one dive, we have not had the many hours of undersea roaming I anticipated, the exhilarating water flights of discovery that thrilled me as a child. I was able to show him an extraordinary marine world that I have found and learned to love, and in that I felt that I was in some small measure repaying him for the great gift he lavished on Philippe and me, the gift of the sea itself.

But there has been something wrong. Though he has intended to join us on many of the dives these past three days, my father has spent long hours in his cabin, working from a briefcase filled with business papers.

At noon on this last day, he boards Alcyone for a special lunch with her crew, and I sit at his side. Midway through the meal, with characteristic bluntness, he admits that he has been experiencing difficulties breathing at depth. It has never happened before, but he understands the problem.

"It is age," he says with a wry smile and a shrug.

During the rendezvous of *Calypso* and *Alcyone*, the Cousteau teams had a chance to pose for a rare group portrait:

1 Michel Verdier
2 Phil McCombs (Washington Post)
3 Francois Sarano
4 Yuki, the dog
5 Bertrand Sion
6 Eric Dayoux
7 Raymond Amaddio
8 Paul Martin

9 Louis Prezelin
10 Anne-Marie Cousteau
11 Jean-Michel Cousteau
12 Captain Jacques-Yves Cousteau
13 Simone Cousteau
14 David Brown
15 Jacques Bellet
16 "Maupiti"
17 Robby Hunter
18 Guy Jouas
19 Yves Zlotnicka
20 Philippe Rueff
21 Mike Westgate

22 Ange Legall
23 Bob Braunbeck
24 Mose Richards
25 Daniel Lemeur
26 Mike Sullivan
27 Chuck Davis
28 Thierry Dupisson
29 Dr. Francois Raineix
30 Thierry Legeunnec
31 Antoine Rosset
32 Marc Le Cavorzin
33 Alain Furic
34 Thierry Stern

The seemingly small difference in water pressure between the regulator, which rides above a diver's back when swimming horizontally, and the lungs is making it difficult to inhale. The lungs are under more pressure than the regulated air supply. In a young person, the extra work required of the lungs is barely noticeable. In an older person, it can be exhausting.

As we finish the meal, I reflect silently on the symbolism of the last few days for my father. Perhaps it has been a great fulfillment and a profound disappointment at the same time. As we toasted one another with champagne, surrounded by dedicated friends and our little flotilla of equipment, I could see that my father was deeply touched. He said we were la force de frappe, a striking force for the environment, and our rendezvous symbolized for him the countless environmentalists around the world who, without vast treasuries or organized armies, go out time and again, obstinately, in old boats or battered jeeps or on foot, to explore nature and to monitor its vitality, to gauge the future of our environmental heritage and to raise their voices over present-day abuses.

And yet, it seemed also to be for him a time of personal reassessment, a time to acknowledge nature's agenda for human bodies. It would not be easy for him, I thought, because he has spent his life refusing to give up. When, as a young man, an automobile accident ended his dream of being a naval aviator and left him partially paralyzed, he struggled for nine months until he was able to move a finger of his left hand. His subsequent entry into the sea came not for science, initially, but for daily therapeutic swims to strengthen his body. When he became fascinated by the sea beneath him, he ignored all the physical limitations of the human and invented a way to swim down into the undersea world like fish.

When lunch is completed, the crews of both ships are assembled on Calypso's foredeck for a group photograph. Phil McCombs and Noirot climb to the top deck to snap a scene that includes Alcyone in the background.

With the event of our rendezvous sealed by the group photo, it is time to move on. Alcyone will leave the lagoon first and sail back to the Sepik. Calypso will head for Manam Island and then Madang.

As I prepare to return to the windship and sail away, my father catches my arm. "I have made a decision about my diving difficulties," he says. I nod silently, waiting to hear him say that he will never dive again. But instead he begins to describe with great animation a new idea for mounting a small air tank on the chest, closer to the lungs, where it would facilitate breathing. I had underestimated the stubborn and boundless spirit of my father, who has overcome every challenge, every disappointment, every tragedy.

"I am going back to Paris," he said, "and invent a new scuba system for old people."

35 Patrick Allioux
36 Joe Guillou
37 Albert Falco
38 Marc Blessington

Not pictured are: Karen Brazeau, Dr. Richard C. Murphy, Jean-Paul Cornu, Don Santee, Patrick Bernard, and Didier Noirot (who took this photograph).

THE LAST SHARK CALLERS

My people on

Manam Island

are happier than

the people living

in Moresby.

The problem is,

they don't know

they're this happy.

Chief Kukura Tibong

The Cousteau amphibious plane *Papagallo* "sails" into the village of Kambaramba, which has been built on stilts in the midst of a waterlogged floodplain along the lower Sepik River.

Midafternoon on Sunday, May 29th, *Alcyone* follows a deep channel, leading out of the Hermit Islands lagoon and points southward, heading back to the Sepik River. Thirty minutes later, *Calypso* follows. Beyond the lagoon, both ships encounter rough seas. *Alcyone*'s nose nearly dips below the water as it slices through waves. *Calypso*'s foredeck is washed by spray that rises as high as the windows of the bridge. The old vessel pitches forward, sways widely. Beams groan. Creaks whisper from every joint. In their quarters, men fasten down loose items. In the *carré*, they shun the food and drink that contributes to seasickness: coffee, tea, orange juice, cola drinks, anything that is highly acidic.

Calypso's heading is south to Manam Island, a sixteen-hour sail. The rough seas persist all night. In their sleeping quarters, the crew nods off among a chorus of familiar sounds: engines droning below, wood squeaking in walls and ceilings, air conditioner humming and gurgling in the hallway between cabins, water crashing outside the portholes, great shudders occasionally vibrating through the ship as it heaves up and smashes forward into a wave. In the common bath, two men stumble back and forth trying to take late-evening showers. Coated in lather that resembles the white clay makeup of island villagers and hopping about to remain standing as the ship tosses rhythmically, they both laugh. "The *Calypso* sing-sing," one says.

J.-M. C.: I stand on the bridge of **Alcyone** *at midnight, sharing the watch with Captain Ruef and Paul Martin as the windship slashes southward through the choppy Bismarck Sea toward the mouth of the Sepik River. Somewhere in the darkness behind us* **Calypso** *labors similarly against the waves. It is a lonely time. Philippe gazes wearily at the instruments. Paul is in the galley making coffee.*

I stare at the navigational chart, which reinforces the feeling that we are far away, in a sparsely traveled sea. Along the bottom I read: "Published London, June 11, 1934, at the Admiralty." Scattered about it are a few corrections and cautions accumulated during the past half-century: "Magnetic disturbance reported in vicinity (1943)." . . . "Hidden reef reported (1944)." . . . "Reported to lie 2 miles W.S.W. from charted position (1942)." In many cases, the latest information on these waters was gathered during World War II, when shipping traffic was briefly intense. For the most part, the seas we travel are imprecisely charted at best.

My mind wanders. What kind of people choose to travel with us out here on the far edges of civilization, dwelling in floating capsules that seldom stop anywhere longer than a day or two, isolated from friends and families back home? The answer, of course, is simply that a few people find happiness in such an unregimented, unpredictable existence. They endure weeks of drudgery and monotony, with the knowledge that soon, perhaps tomorrow, the ship will encounter something unexpected and magical that will compensate for the hardships.

We seem to collect people who find happiness in ranging about the world, who would chafe at the restraints of a sedentary and provincial life. I recall standing on **Calypso**'s *bridge one evening, glancing at the people in the room and thinking about their collective knowledge of the world; my father, who has missed few places in the world; my mother, who as a young girl traveled on steamships between France and the Orient and lived in Japan and Singapore; Bebert, who has spent nearly four decades traveling the world with my parents; Yves Zlotnicka, who was born in Nice to a Russian mother and Dutch father, then educated in Switzerland and Denmark, and now speaks five languages;*

Antoine Rosset, from a patrician family in Paris, who has traveled widely since
an early age and lived in the Philippines; Didier Noirot, who has worked in the
Persian Gulf, the Bahamas, Mexico, Egypt, the Caribbean, and the Maldives.

From all of our different origins, educations, families, interests, experiences,
travels, we have all converged to explore together aboard two sister ships, and
somehow, at this intersection of lives and dreams, we find a measure of
happiness.

Happiness.

What an imposing and complex notion! I think of the villagers we have met on
this expedition, their lives embedded in a world romantically thought of as
Paradise. Surely there is no more universal human fantasy than the idea of
escaping to the carefree, sun-drenched, sea-freshened life of a tropical island
in the South Seas. But the people who are born to this dream, who know little
else of the planet and have few opportunities to travel beyond neighboring
islands: Are they "happy"? Are they fulfilled? Or do they yearn to "escape" to a
faster pace and materially richer world?

We know that these are subjective questions, that contentment and dissatis-
faction shift by degrees from one human mind to the next, yet we are intrigued
by the questions. Sitting in the quiet of Alcyone's *bridge, I resolve to explore this*
idea of "happiness" in Paradise as we wander from island to island during the
next, and last, month of the expedition.

As the sun rises on May 30th, *Calypso* is still three hours from Manam
Island. Chief Engineer Jo Guillou, as handy in a galley as an engine room,
rises early and cooks crepes for the entire crew. As they file into the *carré*
one by one, still sleepy-eyed, the plate of folded crepes draws "ooh-la-la's."
The soft pancakes are opened, spread with jam or marmalade, then rolled
into tubes. The general delight with this surprise is such that when an
excited crew member steps in, pointing in the direction of the bow, saying
"We're approaching Mount Fuji!", the dozen men around the table nod
politely and continue with their genuine French breakfast treat, a homey
comfort after months at sea.

And Manam Island does look from the north side like Mt. Fuji, with its
sheer, triangular shape and cloudy cap. A horn of volcanic ash gives a regal
look to the peak, where a constant gush of smoke wafts into the air. Manam is an active volcano, so marked on the sailing charts, and so defined
by recent history. Of the more than 100 volcanoes in Papua New Guinea,
38 are believed still capable of erupting, and most of these are located in
what is called the Bismarck Volcanic Arc, which ranges from Wewak to
Rabaul, at the southern edges of the Bismarck Sea.

Prezelin and Braunbeck again go aloft in the helicopter when the ship is
within five miles of the coast of Manam. They spend forty minutes
swooping up and down steep mountain walls, wandering to and fro across
the five-mile diameter of the island, hovering over the carbon-gray peak,
which gapes open to the east. There, a river of black gravel winds down to
a black sand beach along the sea, a clue to the continuing fury within
Manam.

For an hour, members of the crew explore the shorelines, inspect the
black ground, and chat with villagers. Just before the first lunch setting,
Guy Jouas receives a call from Dick Murphy. The scientist is on the mainland only ten miles away and proposes to join the ship for a visit to the tiny
island of Boesa, which is three miles off the west coast of Manam. Murphy
believes there is an important story on Boesa.

Murphy brings in tow a Manam native named Michael Boagin, who now works for the provincial government in Madang. Michael is the brother of a Manam chief, was born there, and dedicated his life to helping the islanders of his home after receiving a degree from the University of Papua New Guinea. He has organized joint meetings among the chiefs of the island to foster cooperation, has presented workshops on appropriate technology, has tried to found a trade school on the island, and has sought to attract a Peace Corps volunteer to teach modern trades.

Murphy introduces Michael to Cousteau, and soon a fact of island life has caught the Captain's attention. The people of both Manam and little Boesa have a fresh water problem. The volcanic soil of their islands does not retain freshwater along the surface. There are a few rooftop catchment systems and numerous wells, but water grows scarce during the dry season. Michael explains that seawater penetrates the volcanic soil from below, and rainwater percolates down from above. Consequently, the less-dense rainwater forms a thin underground layer, or lens, floating on the seawater. To extract this tiny "reservoir" of fresh water, people go to the shore, dig holes in the sand, and wait for the tide to rise so that the floating freshwater lens is raised closer to the surface. With growing populations and a difficult water situation, the islands face an uncertain future.

On a previous visit to Manam, Murphy has learned of this dilemma, and has researched appropriate-technology solutions at the University of Hawaii. "The island of Hawaii is a volcano with water problems and, by comparison, immense financial resources to search for solutions," he explains. "What better place to look for information to help Manam?"

Murphy shows Cousteau a letter he has written to the chief of Manam Island, proposing some ideas on behalf of The Cousteau Society, after consultations with other experts. First, there should be a geological/hydrographic survey to determine how much water is being retained beneath the soil in the freshwater lens. Knowing that this can be expensive for the islanders, Murphy has offered to help seek financial support. Secondly, should the tests prove positive, Murphy provides the chief with documentation on several systems developed for other tropical islands with water problems, including solar-powered (photovoltaic) pumps.

He tells the chief: "The fewer moving parts, the lower the capital expenditure, and the less fuel consumed the better." Solar pumps, once installed, use the free services of nature, and, though the pumps have moving parts, the photovoltaic systems do not. There are more than 1,000 such systems in operation throughout the South Pacific, he reports, and the literature suggests that they work well.

Calypso crosses a small strait and anchors near the only village on the tiny island of Boesa. Boagin tells the team that about 500 people live on the island and that their only sources of fresh water are the rain, which is caught on specially built roofs that drain into holding tanks, and a spring so tiny it does not flow but drips inside a small cave. To reach the spring, island women must follow a steep trail to the far side of the island.

Cousteau, Murphy, and Boagin climb from the shore to a plateau with scattered huts, where Phillip Gabuzi, the chief, waits with a hastily organized dance troupe to welcome the visitors. He takes them to see the communal rainwater tanks, the spigots of which are locked to prevent poaching. Above the tanks, in a small cabin, there is a sophisticated reverse osmosis desalination system, purchased with a government grant.

Dancers welcome Captain Cousteau to tiny Boesa Island, near Manam, where *Calypso*'s team ran hoses from the ship to help fill villagers' freshwater tanks. Like many tropical islands, volcanic soils on Boesa and Manam do not retain water efficiently.

A *singsing* dancer performs during a party welcoming both *Calypso* and *Alcyone* to the north coast town of Madang. In Papua New Guinea, the presence of two renowned ships evoked fascination in some towns but little more than puzzlement in places where neither Cousteau television programs nor books had ever appeared.

Unfortunately, neither the desalination system nor the pump to draw in seawater is working. No one on the island has any knowledge of how to maintain or repair the machinery, and there is no money to hire a repairman, if indeed someone with the training can be found in Papua New Guinea.

Cousteau contacts *Calypso* by walkie-talkie and summons Jo Guillou and Thierry le Guennec to look over the equipment in case the two engineers could fix it.

After half an hour, Guillou pronounces the pump irreparable. The desalination unit requires special parts that would have to be ordered from the United States. Shaking their heads, the engineers marvel at the unit. It is the same system installed aboard *Calypso*, but a more expensive, larger model.

Boagin waves at the system in disgust. "It is like giving the Space Shuttle to Papua New Guinea!" he says. "What are they going to do with it?"

Cousteau has an idea. Though there is little more the team can do to repair the island's "inappropriate technology," they can leave a few days' supply of fresh water behind as a gift. He calls Falco and asks that the crew run a hose from the ship to the island and fill a tank with fresh water from *Calypso*. Presently, Eric Dayou and Maupiti stand on a bluff at the island's edge, filling buckets that are carried on the heads of youngsters and dumped into the tank. Sensing the gaiety of the young people over this break in village routine, the two men occasionally whip the hose about to spray the carriers, a welcome refreshment in the heat and a playful act that elicits joyful screams and laughter. Perhaps it is the first time fresh water has been abundant enough on Boesa Island to be a source of frivolity.

When the visit is over, and the Zodiacs are being loaded aboard, Le Gal tosses plastic bottles of spring water to youngsters in dugouts at *Calypso*'s stern. "The water will be consumed quickly," he says, "but the bottles will be used indefinitely as canteens."

Watching children scramble for the bottles, Captain Cousteau reflects on the water situation. "Let's be entirely honest with ourselves," he tells Boagin and Murphy. "Water *is* available, although it is limited and difficult to obtain. Like any other renewable resource, it can support only so many people. When the demand exceeds the supply, the normal human response is to look elsewhere for a culprit. In this case, people say there isn't enough water. But if we look at it from another perspective, it is possible to conclude that there are too many consumers rather than too little water."

Murphy recalls a discussion he had on Manam with people who were lamenting the increasing problem of overcrowding. He asked if there was a family-planning program to control population growth. The response was that such a thing would be impossible on Manam since ninety percent of the villagers were Catholics.

At 6:00 P.M., the ship hoists anchor and sets out for Madang. In the carré, over dinner, Murphy tells Cousteau about a meeting he has had with Kukura Tibong, a chief on Manam. Murphy was interested in learning how the villagers view the outside world. There had been a few tourists on the island, backpackers for the most part, and the traditional hospitality had been extended. Singsings were held, some local gifts given. The villagers had been impressed by some articles the visitors possessed: instant cameras, wristwatches, Swiss Army knives. The first few times tourists came, the village considered the visits to be grand events. But gradually, the villagers realized that they were sharing their culture and going to some lengths to entertain the visitors, but they were getting nothing in return. Kukura Tibong seemed unsure what position to take regarding the development of tourism in Papua New Guinea, something most people in the government favor.

Some young villagers, the chief told Murphy, had gone to Port Moresby for work or education, and they had chosen to remain in that world of cars and houses and interesting things. The chief said he hoped for some development on Manam Island. Murphy asked what changes he envisioned.

"Having more things and some stores and having some economic activity here," said Kukura Tibong.

"OK. Do you consider the people in Port Moresby to be living in a developed environment?" asked Murphy.

"Absolutely."

"Do you think the people in Moresby are happier than the people on this island?"

"Oh, no. Not at all," said the chief. "My people on Manam Island are happier than the people living in Moresby. The problem is, they don't know they're this happy."

As the discussion continued, the chief agreed with Murphy that what he needed was a kind of "appropriate" development—better medical care, electricity, water pumps, education, for example. Other aspects of the modern world, imported to Manam, would probably have a negative impact on the island in the long run.

As he left the island, Murphy tells Cousteau, he realized that the concept of "development" in the minds of many villagers was about as vague and unrealistic as the Western concept of "Paradise." Perhaps the only solution, the chief and Murphy agreed, was a new educational program in which former island residents now living in the city could teach villagers about the long-range implications of development.

After a night sail, *Calypso* enters Madang harbor at sunrise. An hour later, *Alcyone* arrives from her brief journey up the mouth of the Sepik to the waterlogged village of Kambaramba, where people live in huts built on stilts. As the two ships tie up together, Jean-Michel boards *Calypso* to tell his father of the filming done in Kambaramba. He is ecstatic, describing how village men race their dugouts, standing erect in the canoes, performing amazing feats of balance. *Papagallo* landed on the river, he says, and floated among the stilt-huts, creating a strange image for the cameras.

The two vessels are welcomed to Madang by Peter Barter, owner of the cruise ship *Melanesian Explorer* and the Madang Resort Hotel. He provides dock space alongside his ship at the edge of the hotel grounds, hosts a local singsing for the crews in the afternoon and a party in the hotel restaurant in the evening.

Calypso's filming mission is now complete. In three days she will leave Madang to carry out a scientific study of the discharge of the Sepik River into the sea, then sail on to Singapore. *Alcyone* will remain in Papua New Guinea during the month of June, then sail to Australia. Several crew members will go home now from Madang, some will shift from one ship to the other. Accordingly, the work of redistributing equipment and personal gear goes on throughout the day.

When time allows, team members walk into Madang, a town of 20,000 built on a peninsula that juts out into a lovely bay. If tourism grows in Papua New Guinea, the luxurious gardens and lawns of Madang and its myriad waterways and tiny harbor islands will probably make the town a mecca for visitors seeking tropical beauty and resort accommodations. Flowering shrubs and trees line the town streets, and alongside them walk girls wearing red hibiscus blooms in their hair and women carrying colorful parasols for shade.

J.-M. C.: This evening, after a welcoming cocktail party, complete with warm speeches by Madang Province Premier Andrew Ariako, my father, and Peter Barter, our entire team is treated to an elegant meal in Peter's hotel restaurant. Sitting with my family, Peter recounts his twenty-five-year history in Papua New Guinea.

Born in Fiji to a family with a chain of department stores in Australia, Peter followed his youthful craving for adventure to the rugged coasts and valleys of Papua New Guinea. He was a pilot for several years, then manager of the domestic airlines Talair. He and his wife Jan began taking tourists up the Sepik River aboard two dugout canoes lashed together with a plank floor across them. The cabin was fashioned of a tent, showers were carried out with a bucket, but the food was good and hardy travelers enjoyed the intimacy with nature, the unexpected encounters.

But the Barter empire is about to expand dramatically, in anticipation of the escalation of tourism predicted by Peter. Presently about 8,000 people vacation here, he tells us. Peter believes that number will jump to 60,000 within five years as tourism from Japan increases. So confident is he that he is building two new ships for luxury tours and a hotel complex in Port Moresby.

As Peter talks, I think about the future as he envisions it. We have many misgivings about large-scale tourism invading the world's last wild places, potentially overwhelming with pollution and crowds the delicate habitats that lure the tourists in the first place, often destroying what Lawrence Durrell called "the spirit of place" and one of our friends, writer Paula DiPerna, has described as "an elusive, ephemeral quality that makes a place feel as it feels, seem as it seems." Tourism can also create local resentments, as well-equipped, wealthy travelers become a permanent fixture among people struggling to make a living, and doing so by becoming servants of the foreigners.

Yet Peter Barter seems to me a businessman who remains sensitive to these issues. He is a naturalized citizen genuinely interested in Papua New Guinea's potential environmental problems and has taken measures to help bring appropriate technology to the country. He is experimenting with the use of solar energy and has helped villagers on Iwa Island install a solar-powered pump to increase their freshwater supplies. He seems an explorer as much as an entrepreneuur and has generously helped our expedition, arranging free office space in Port Moresby for Karen Brazeau, making available to us James Kinjimali, who is a guide on the **Melanesian Explorer** *and served in the same role during Alcyone's Sepik voyage.*

The question is, of course, will all of the tourism operators in Papua New Guinea's future be Peter Barters? If huge resorts arrive, will they be controlled by local people or international corporations concerned only about profit margins; will the reefs suffer, as Hawaii's have, and pollution clog the harbors, as in the Greek Isles? Will all singsings become stale, paid performances for tourists? Will the solace and replenishment offered by remote tropical islands be shattered by the crowds of people seeking this peacefulness of Paradise but bringing with them the frenzies they dream of escaping? And, most importantly, will the local people walk among the tourists with dignity, or will they be treated, and thus feel, like second-class citizens in their own country?

Overleaf: In Kambaramba, children learn at an early age to travel and play in canoes, quickly becoming so adept they can paddle while standing. Unable to raise sufficient food in the surrounding swamps, Kambaramba has sustained itself over the years with a unique barter system. In exchange for goods from other villages, Kambaramba operates several brothels.

Late in the afternoon of June 1st, *Calypso* sets out from Madang for the mouth of the Sepik. Aboard now are Dr. Lewis Fox and Richard Ouellet from Harvard University, and Dr. Patrick Osborne and Robin Totome from the University of Papua New Guinea. With Dick Murphy and Cousteau Society aides David Brown and Tim Trabon, the scientists will gather data with several research objectives in mind: first, to obtain an overview of estuary bathymetry and river flow; then to measure and evaluate a number of physical, chemical, and biological characteristics upstream, in the estuary, and offshore from the river's discharge; to examine the relationships between some river minerals; and finally, to quantify the contribution of nitrogen and phosphorus made by the Sepik to the ocean.

The studies are a continuation of a broad analysis of the world's major rivers conducted jointly by The Cousteau Society, Harvard's Center for Earth and Planetary Sciences, and local scientific institutions. Reports have already been completed on the Amazon and Mississippi.

The purpose is to arrive at a better understanding of the effect large river systems have on the vitality of the ocean, since, as Captain Cousteau has observed, rivers are the "roots of the sea" and thus critically important to global oceanic and atmospheric processes. Over geological time scales, the seas have been fertilized by nitrogen and phosphorus carried from the continents to the sea by rivers. To gauge the contributions of various rivers, the teams study the characteristics of the interface of fresh and salt waters. The interest goes far beyond the discharge of a single river, since, on a planetary basis, the amount of terrestrial nutrients entering the sea can affect ocean primary productivity and thus the fixation of carbon dioxide into organic matter. Since atmospheric carbon dioxide influences climate through the greenhouse effect, uptake by the oceans is potentially important on a global scale. The researchers hope to contribute to a better understanding of the vast chemistry of the oceans and climate, at a time when scientists harbor growing anxieties that delicate balances may be threatened by human impacts, conjuring up the worrisome scenario of great climatic changes.

Arriving at the Sepik plume, the team confronts a dramatic marine setting: the river's outflow retains its deep brown color for a short distance, then, as sediments settle out, the water turns an opaque green from phytoplankton fueled by the Sepik's cargo of nutrients. Laid out before the scientists is a living cross section of the marine food chain. The plankton serves as a food source for a diversity of sea life, including bait fish which are, in turn, preyed upon by birds and tuna. Raining down to deeper water, the plankton also feed bottom-dwellers. At the fertile boundary between the plume and the ocean, the team sees the final trophic level, as islanders catch fish, ultimately nourished by rich volcanic soils from hundreds of miles inland where the Sepik washes the slopes of the central mountains.

When the plume study is completed, Murphy and Osborne fly in *Papagallo* to join *Alcyone*'s team, which is exploring Long Island, the crown of an underwater volcano located some thirty miles off the north coast of Papua New Guinea.

Some 300 years ago, Long Island appears to have been the site of a cataclysmic volcanic eruption, one of the greatest of the last thousand years. Yet because of its remoteness, the eruption occurred without the knowledge of Europeans. In a recent book, *The Time of Darkness*, geologist Russell Blong recounts his exploration of thin layers of inorganic

Vessels from two different worlds cross the point where Sepik River water mixes with seawater off the northern coast of Papua New Guinea. Scientists aboard *Calypso* studied the Sepik plume to measure the volume of essential nutrients, derived from rich volcanic soils, contributed by the freshwater system to the ocean.

An aerial view of tiny Motmot Island, a miniature volcano that has arisen in Lake Wisdom, which is the flooded caldera of Long Island, itself a volcano surrounded by water. Cousteau scientists contributed to a long-term study seeking to learn how life gradually arrives on Motmot, barren when it first arose from the lake in the 1960s.

sediments across a wide swath of the Papua New Guinea mainland, which lead him to conclude that the Long Island explosion was equal in magnitude to the eruption of Krakatau in 1883 and perhaps more than four times larger than the eruption of Vesuvius, which buried Pompeii in 79 A.D.

Traveling from village to village, Blong found more than fifty distinct but closely related legends passed down through several generations, all of which described a "time of darkness," when great clouds blocked the sun and ash rained down from the sky for days. The tales describe a desperate period, when crops died and starvation spread through the villages. When the event had passed, however, the land seemed newly fertilized and more productive, a likely effect of the volcano's widespread dissemination of mineral-rich clouds of ash.

Over the centuries, the caldera of Long Island has filled with water, forming a body of fresh water known as Lake Wisdom. Eruptions in the 1960s thrust a new crater through the surface of the lake, creating a tiny island now bearing the name Motmot. It is a miniature volcano surrounded by water, within a volcano surrounded by water.

In 1969, two scientists—Eldon Ball and Jean-Marie Bassot—came upon Motmot and realized that they had found a "ready-made laboratory for studying biological colonization and succession." They had discovered a tiny fragment of earth at the very beginning of its biological history, a microcosm of a new world. If they merely let time pass and revisited Motmot occasionally, they could keep a kind of scientific diary that might answer several questions: What gets to the island and how? What succeeds, what does not, and why?

The Cousteau team, fascinated by this study, has arranged to gather samples of life presently on Motmot to aid the continuing project. When *Papagallo* sets down on Lake Wisdom, the team looks out upon an otherworldly scene: a rim of steep, 200-foot cliffs surround the lake, which is about two miles across and contains, in the center, the moonscape fragment called Motmot. As the men step from the plane into knee-deep water, they are startled by the variation in temperature: scalding water at the knees but cooler water only a few inches below. Rushing ashore onto Motmot, they must jump a steaming strip of sand at the waterline, which measures 190 degrees Fahrenheit, evidence of the continuing volcanic activity that created the little island.

Cousteau marine biologist Dr. Richard Murphy (in white) and Dr. Patrick Osborne of the University of Papua New Guinea explore Motmot, gathering samples of its plant life.

Over the years, Ball and Bassot had followed the gradual introduction of life on Motmot, a process perhaps similar to the arrival of organisms on other newly formed islands around the world. Initially, they found three or four immature plants and two clumps of sedge, which they reasoned were brought to the island as seeds clinging to the feathers or feet of a few black ducks that had begun to nest on Motmot. Eventually, mosses and ferns arrived, their spores probably carried on the wind or in the droppings of birds, which were briefly stopping on the island. The first invertebrates to arrive were lycosid spiders, either blown by wind or rafted on floating vegetation. Perhaps in similar ways, the next wave of creatures appeared: earwigs, beetles, and ants.

Murphy and Osborne roam the island for several hours collecting samples. They find some empty bird nests, one with decayed but unbroken eggs in it, leading them to wonder what might have driven away or killed the birds. Along the shore, they measure chemical constituents issuing from thermal vents and collect snails, worms, and insect larvae in the water. Sorting through their assemblage of sample plants and insects, the two scientists do not find any new arrivals since the last visit of Ball and Bassot several years before. Though their collection does not contain any surprises, it does illustrate the slow pace by which life is dispersed across geographic barriers, ultimately to settle and to colonize even the most alien islands.

From Long Island, *Alcyone* ranges northeast through the Bismarck Sea, anchoring wherever the team suspects a reef might offer good diving. Prezelin and Davis have moved from *Calypso* to the windship, and during the next five days they accumulate more underwater footage—black-tip sharks, large sea turtles, more legions of dazzling reef fish.

While the windship is engaged in random explorations, Dick Murphy has flown to the island of New Ireland. The team hopes to find and to film here an ancient tradition called "shark calling," in which villagers in canoes reportedly summon up sharks using rituals and incantations and employing rattles to attract the sharks, which are then caught with a rope noose. Murphy has decided to search for one of these skilled fishermen.

For several days, Murphy travels about trying to find a shark caller. He works under some pressure, since *Alcyone*'s permit to remain in the country will expire in three weeks, and Jean-Michel has composed a long list of sites to visit and stories to film before the windship and its crew must depart Papua New Guinea.

Murphy has been given the name Selam Karasibe, said to be a well-known shark caller in Kontu, but when he arrives Selam cannot be found. The elders of the village, however, happen to be gathered in a council meeting. Murphy and his guide introduce themselves, and the scientist makes a long presentation describing the Cousteau mission. Finally, he asks if anyone would be willing to perform the fishing method so that it can be documented on film.

There is a measure of ambivalence in the community. On the one hand, the men want their traditions protected from massive exploitation. Some things lose power when they're shared or publicized. On the other hand, they are proud of their culture and want it recognized and even preserved on film.

The elders fall into a long discussion of the pros and cons. Their answer, after twenty minutes have passed, is roughly: "Thank you. Nice to meet you. We don't want to do it."

Periodically cataloguing the plant and animal life that appears on Motmot, scientists learn about the process by which land forms acquire their unique ecosystems. Here, plant spores and seeds are carried across water on the feet or in the stomachs of birds and by wind gusts. Spiders, insects, and even some small mammals can come aboard rafts of organic matter floating in the surrounding water or on the wind.

However, the decision is a general response from the community, they explain. If an individual in the village wants to help Murphy, fine.

Back to looking for Selam. Someone thinks he may be at a medical center some three hours back up the road Murphy has come down. The scientist and his less-than-enthusiastic guide make the return trip only to find that Selam has already left the medical center for Kavieng. Off to Kavieng. En route, the guide spots Selam in a passing pickup and hails the vehicle.

Selam is happy to oblige, but he can't settle on a price. Murphy realizes that it's Friday night, and Selam has been celebrating. Further discussion will have to wait until the effects of drink wear off the next morning. The scientist drives back to Kavieng, meets *Alcyone*, and instructs the crew to meet him the next morning at Kontu, an easy sail down the southern coast of the island.

But the next morning, Selam's condition, reinforced during the night, has not changed radically. He is able to describe the techniques of shark calling, but he is twenty-four hours from being sound enough to carry them out. Murphy resolves to remain with the fisherman in the Kontu mens' house until the next morning, in hopes of encouraging temperance through the afternoon and night.

A Kontu villager on New Ireland shows Cousteau biologist Dr. Richard Murphy the roots of a vine belonging to the *Derris* family. Along inland streams and shallow ocean reefs, some Papua New Guinea villagers capture fish by loading up the water with rotenone, a substance they pound from *Derris* roots. The chemical paralyzes the respiratory system of fish. The process is similar to a tribal fishing technique witnessed by the Cousteau team along the Amazon river.

Cousteau divers found
extraordinary scenes
of beauty and diversity
in many parts of
Papua New Guinea's
little-explored and
untouched waters.
The tiny fish in this
photo, taken off Cape
St. George along
New Ireland Island,
are basslets.

At 4:00 A.M., the scientist is treated to the New Ireland equivalent of an alarm clock. Lying in a bamboo cot, he first hears lone rooster calls, then a chorus of roosters. Next, a family of pigs passes the hut, grunting and snorting. Songbirds follow about 5:00 A.M., then a village woman begins to sing. Fifteen minutes later, a flock of crows rises from nearby trees and flies overhead squawking. At 6:00 A.M., since it is now Sunday morning, a recording of church music comes drifting through the village.

At last Murphy's organizational marathon seems finished. Selam awakens ready to begin the rituals that lead to shark calling. Murphy accompanies him to the shore and watches him set to work. What might appear to outsiders as a show of manliness is in fact a highly spiritual endeavor for islanders. Selam's first act is to drop stones on the fringing reef and to strike it with a spear. This is meant to call the shark spirits and to alert them that the caller is about to venture out to contact them.

Next, Selam paddles his outrigger offshore, where he begins to shake a coconut-shell rattle on the surface. If a shark approaches, he will quickly drop a vine hoop to lasso the fish, setting off a violent struggle.

The problem is: no sharks come. Selam works with his rattle all morning, and the Cousteau film team sits in a Zodiac nearby under the hot sun ready to capture footage of the battle from above and below the water, to no avail. For six days, the same ritual is conducted by Selam, and the team waits, and no shark appears.

On June 19th, with no footage yet captured of Selam catching a shark, the team decides to spend one more day pursuing the story before sailing on. In midafternoon, Selam signals the team that a shark is approaching.

A successful "shark caller" heads for home with his catch. On several Papua New Guinea islands, fishermen use coconut-shell rattles to attract ("call") sharks and vine lassoes to pull them in.

Shark-calling can be a perilous means of obtaining food if a fisherman is not careful. Violent struggles often ensue when a shark is caught in a fisherman's hoop. To be certain his catch will not continue its battle when pulled into the small outrigger, the captor dispatches the creature with a hardwood club.

Prezelin and Davis roll their cameras and film a spectacular scene of the shark caller struggling with a shark in the vine noose, at last rolling the exhausted fish into his canoe. Only an hour before giving up, the team has their story on film. The day ends with Selam returning in triumph to Kontu, where everyone seems gratified that their ancient art has been shown effective. When *Alcyone* is ready to depart, scores of villagers paddle out in outriggers to wave good-bye, and Selam comes aboard to present his shark calling rattles to the team as a farewell gift.

J.-M. C.: A few days later, when I join **Alcyone** *for our final missions in Papua New Guinea, Dick Murphy tells me a touching story, one that evokes the subtle notions of "happiness" in this changing culture.*

When it was time to make one last trip back over the road from Kontu to Kavieng, Murphy asked if any villagers needed a ride. Two young New Ireland men accepted the offer. As they set out, facing three hours in an automobile, Dick realized that he had been relentlessly asking questions about their culture. Perhaps they had some questions about his world, and if so, he would try to answer them during this long drive.

"What is it like living in cities rather than in the forest?" they wondered.

Murphy described a day in his life at home: rushing to work in a river of automobiles, the sounds and smells and the smog, eating frequently in crowded restaurants, hurrying to complete paperwork and phone calls so that he could rush back home again amid the cars. He compared the support systems of city and forest, explaining that his highly developed world was addicted to petroleum, and if the supply were ever interrupted or exhausted, there would be massive disruptions. "In that regard," he said, "my world is not nearly as stable as yours, no matter how it looks from afar."

Murphy asked what they thought of the great changes heading their way, the arrival of new products and new ways of life.

The young men found it difficult to answer. Generally, they imagine that these new things will be very good, and everyone they know wants them. It is clear to Murphy that the vast potential for deleterious effects as materialism pervades the cherished traditions and the delicate ecology of the islands has never occurred to these bright, inquisitive young men.

"What do you think of outsiders like me, of white people?" Murphy asks.

"White people are very clever."

"You mean they are manipulative, they take advantage of people?"

"No, I mean they are very bright. They can do a lot of things."

The tone of envy in the voices of the young islanders upsets Dick.

Having spent the past few months with village people, sleeping in their thatched houses, eating their food, and learning about their customs, Murphy has come to appreciate the knowledge embodied in their culture. Thus, the young men's comment evokes an explosive response from him. Yes, the foreigners know how a city works, how to earn money, how to use machines, how to solve problems in a "developed" system because they have grown up there. They know the city ecosystem, know the subtle cues and the language of the city.

But, Dick says, put those same people in the forest and they are completely helpless. They have no idea how to survive in the bush. In Papua New Guinea, on the other hand, villagers know the languages and cues of the forest system, know when and where to fish, to hunt, to gather, where to step, what to touch, what to eat and what not to eat. You know the medicines of the forest and the reefs, he tells them. You know the plant to cure ringworm, the ones to prevent gonorrhea, the one to stop diarrhea. You know the quality and uses of the wood in every tree, the best vines to make rope, how to make a flexible bamboo bed. You have traditions that protect these living resources for the future, and you care enough about your ancestors and the future generations to abide by the rules of your culture.

During the drive, Murphy had begun playing an audiocassette that featured some of his favorite classical pieces—Tchaikovsy, Mozart, Beethoven. The young men loved the music. When the tape finished, they asked that it be played again, and in the course of the long drive it was repeated again and again. They never tired of this new music. (Weeks later, Murphy sent them the tape from Los Angeles. As they listened, they opened a pandanus-leaf basket and shared their food with Murphy—turtle meat caught by the father of one young man, some taro cooked in coconut milk, sweet potatoes.

Listening to Murphy, I think about the rare and valuable moments these three strangers shared, educating one another about their different solutions to survival, about the diversity of human life and the common architecture of the human mind and heart. For me, the story is highly symbolic. Those young men, bored by the pleasures provided by their world, imagine that "happiness" lies in those cities on distant horizons, while those of us unsatisfied in those cities

A young villager on Long Island, off Papua New Guinea's northern coast, gazes at nature's twilight spectacle from his outrigger canoe. Though television has reached some parts of the country, most youngsters still find their entertainment in natural materials and events, as well as the dramatic stories told by elders.

imagine that life on a distant isle in the blue sea must be idyllic and resounding with "happiness." I sometimes wonder if happiness exists at all outside the yearning for happiness.

Perhaps it is mostly a matter of our abilities to perceive and appreciate passing moments of joy, and if Murphy helped fuel in those young men a greater pride and appreciation for their ways and their environment, maybe he led them to perceive a measure of "happiness" they simply had not recognized.

It seems that a physical setting can facilitate happiness, but it cannot ensure it. It is our responsibility to identify and to treasure the moments of potential happiness as they appear in our lives. For me, and for those of us on Alcyone *and* Calypso, *the moments of discovery, profound or trivial, are great sources of pleasure. Perhaps my friend Murphy and two young men from New Ireland will cherish as a time of great happiness three sublime hours spent bouncing over a rough road listening to classical music, eating from a pandanus basket, and discovering some of the innermost details of their equally mysterious worlds.*

THE PRICE OF TREES AND WHALES

WE, THE PEOPLE OF

PAPUA NEW GUINEA

—United in one nation—

pay homage to the

memory of our

ancestors—the source

of our strength and origin

of our combined heritage

—acknowledge the

worthy customs and

traditional wisdoms of

our people—which have

come down to us from

generation to generation

—pledge ourselves to

guard and pass on to

those who come after us

our noble traditions and

the Christian principles

that are ours now.

From the Preamble,

Papua New Guinea

Constitution

Fishermen along the southwest
coast of New Ireland fasten
slings of surgical rubber
to their spears. The "guns"
are more powerful than hand
spears but larger fish have become
wary of them and often stay away.

On the top floor of the PNG Building, one of many high rise office and apartment structures that have changed the skyline of Port Moresby in recent times, an elevator opens before the dark hardwood doors of a renowned and exclusive institution in Papua New Guinea called the Papua Club. The doors are ornately carved with traditional designs, and they lead into a spacious lounge with bar, sitting areas, an outdoor barbeque terrace, and a poolroom with two immense snooker tables. The wood paneling is rich, the carpets plush, the view of Port Moresby harbor exalting. Political power brokers and business executives from Papua New Guinea's largest concerns stand at the Club bar sipping South Pacific draught. It is clear from the conversations and the masculine atmosphere that the Papua Club serves as a bastion for the male elite of the capital city.

The Papua Club has offered British and Australian men a home away from home for seventy-five years. Throughout most of that history, Papua New Guinea nationals were not admitted to membership, although prominent native-born physicians or businessmen could visit as guests. With the coming of independence, a new cadre of young national politicians and businessmen has arisen, and with the nation's future resting in black hands, the Papua Club opted to change its membership guidelines. Now, a handful of nationals are officers and members of the Club, welcome to mingle with prominent expats gathered above the streets of Port Moresby.

Club rules safeguard privacy and ensure a relaxed, manly atmosphere. It is against house rules to talk within the Club's confines of business matters, even to pass along one's business card. Women are allowed to enter the Club only four times each year during formal affairs. Prominently displayed on a small desk is the Rooney Book, in which wagers of any kind that occur at the Club bar are recorded. In 1951, for example, one Club member bet another that General Eisenhower would not last as Supreme Commander of Allied Powers in Europe (SCAPE) for another three months.

The atmosphere seems anomalous in the midst of Papua New Guinea's emancipated society and politics, as if a relic of the old colonial empire were encased in glass at the top of a building, and yet the clubby male membership bears an interesting resemblance to the gatherings of male elders in the village *haus tambaran*, where betel nuts serve the same function as beer and where a woman's life could be in danger were she to breach the sanctity of the ancient men's "club" to peek brazenly at the sacred flutes or the *garamut*.

Since business is a taboo subject, talk centers on the national passion, rugby. There is enormous pride in the Papua New Guinea national team, which has played around the world and has recently defeated the highly rated Australian team twice, a source of great inspiration to citizens of a tiny, developing nation.

When the notion of independence began to dominate conversations at the Club bar twenty years ago, there were some expats who believed the nation would turn into a vast and violent primitive tribe if handed over to nationals. The fear has proven completely unfounded, and the new leaders in Papua New Guinea's government and industry have tended to adopt the business practices, dress codes, and sports of Western culture while maintaining a vocal pride in their heritage. They talk rugby, play snooker, belong to the local golf club, gather at the South Pacific Beer Company VIP Lounge for special celebrations. (It is a source of pride among nationals in the capital that a brewery owned by Heineken and shipped here piece by piece from Germany is overseen by a native-born master brewer.)

As they drive about Port Moresby in late-model Japanese cars, the new leaders of the nation are surrounded by symbols of Papua New Guinea's aggregation of past and future. The metropolitan area includes more than half a dozen villages, where people still live in huts and stilt-houses.

Some of these villagers commute to work in high rise commercial buildings and hotels, where they pass through concrete facades based on ancient artwork into modern offices and hotel suites. The offices are outfitted with computers, telex, and fax machines; the hotel rooms may feature a telephone in the bathroom and a television set in the living room, where it is possible, in the evening, to watch the *Today* show live from New York City.

Amid these cultural warps in the capital city, the new leaders of Papua New Guinea wrestle with the nation's future—pondering how to import new ideas and technology without obliterating the ways of the ancestors; how to profit from the country's natural resources without destroying luxurious ecosystems that continue to sustain millions of outlying citizens; how to run a nation efficiently that encompasses more than seven hundred languages, nineteen provincial regions of widely varying natures, and hundreds of villages bent on preserving their own independence and obeying only the word of the local "big man."

One result of this maze of problems is a bureaucracy that sometimes seems to be spinning its wheels. After months of frustrating delays and red tape in her efforts to secure expedition authorizations from dozens of offices in Moresby, Karen Brazeau realizes one day that she is in the position of dealing with an "adolescent" government. Like any thirteen-year-old, it is having trouble coping with growth, with new emotions and responsibilities, with worries about its future, with peer pressures, and with advice and continuing influence from the elder nations responsible for its birth and its characteristics.

J.-M. C.: During our journeys through Papua New Guinea, we have visited sites where crucial decisions that will shape the nation's future are being made. When I heard Karen's metaphor of a thirteen-year-old undergoing an inevitable maturing process, it struck me that this image of an adolescent can be taken a step further. The young nation has inherited a vast natural fortune and must now educate itself intensely in order to manage this wealth in the wisest way. The riches could be squandered or lost to outsiders, or they could be husbanded and invested to sustain the nation far into the future.

The most obvious of Papua New Guinea's exploitable treasures are its living funds of vegetation and wildlife. Though crocodile and butterfly farms now exist, far greater profits may be derived from the woods of the nation's vast rain forests and the living bounty of its encircling seas.

But there are two enormous challenges to anyone who would try to turn these resources into cash. The first is simply to devise ways of extracting massive quantities of timber or sea life without disrupting the fragile webs of nature they help to support. The other is to exploit the forests and fisheries in new ways without eliminating the traditional resources of local people. To proceed with rapid exploitation before finding solutions to these problems is to jeopardize the environmental legacy of Papua New Guinea's future generations.

During our Land Team's travels through the interior of the country, they stopped at the largest forestry operation in Papua New Guinea, a project some view as a model for large-scale exploitation of the nation's forests. The opera-

tion, called JANT, is located near Madang along the north coast of the mainland. The major shareholder in the company is the Honshu Paper Company of Japan, and the product is wood chips for the manufacture of paper and fine tissue in Japan. In 1974, the company began harvesting timber on a 210,000-acre tract.

Initially, the project seems to have been welcomed by most people in the area. Hopes were high that substantial compensation payments would be made to local landowning villages; that tree cutting would open space for gardens and provide roads and other benefits such as schools and medical facilities. The management of JANT points proudly to the 340 miles of road constructed within the area, maintaining that this network serves as a lifeline for the daily needs of local people. The project also employs some 500 nationals.

After logging the native forest, some thirteen species of fast-growing trees were planted to establish a continually renewing supply of timber. Where such planting was deemed undesirable, the company planted coffee and cocoa trees and established agricultural fields.

However, while our Land Team was visiting the region, and during an earlier reconnaissance trip by Dick Murphy, local villagers expressed great disappointment in the operation. Our people were told that reforestation had not proceeded as originally planned and that the Madang Provincial government has banned any similar logging projects pending a complete reevaluation.

The feelings of many local villagers may have been expressed by a man named Wezip Aloloum, who testified about the unexpected effects of JANT on his land:

The machines dug up the ground and now the soil has lost its goodness. . . . If I plant banana, sweet potato, or taro, they will not grow well. The leaves will be yellow. . . . I planted some coffee. I also planted some cocoa . . . but they did not grow well. . . . There are no goura pigeon, cassowary, bird of paradise, and wallaby left. . . . I would not like my grandchildren, or their grandchildren after them, to be short of wildlife and to say "Father did not think of those of us who were coming later. He thought only of himself, and finished off all the birds and animals, so that now I have none."

Our Land Team cinematographer Jean-Paul Cornu showed me a letter from the JANT management to a group of schoolchildren in Sweden who had written to protest the project. The company expressed their concerns for the region and described their efforts to minimize the environmental impact of the operation. The sentiments appeared genuine, but one sentence stood out as I read the letter: "We would like you to understand," they told the children, "that this country is not a botanical garden nor zoo called 'Papua,' but a developing independent country called Papua New Guinea, with more than three million people and a population which is increasing every year."

So often in our travels through developing countries we have come across the assumption that the environment and progress are at odds and that the perceived needs of impoverished and expanding human populations must take precedence. It invariably serves as an excuse to trade a parcel of nature evolved over millions of years, woven of organic linkages that can never be reconstructed, for quick profits. Sometimes the economic gains provide a temporary stimulus to the local standard of living, and sometimes the benefits accrue only to faraway shareholders with no knowledge of their impact.

Either way, the long-term result is usually a deterioration in the vitality of a productive ecosystem and a severe decline in the quality of human life locally.

Equipped with a chain saw, a local logger fells a mammoth hardwood tree near Angoram, along the lower Sepik River. In contrast to large commercial timber companies, now threatening some forested areas of Papua New Guinea by clear-cutting, the man pictured here is part of a village cooperative that removes trees selectively, causing minimal disruption to the ecological balance of the forest. Small sawmills set up among the trees allow villagers to process the wood on the site. Planks are sold only to other villages in the region. Men take turns using communal equipment, and the proceeds from this local enterprise are shared throughout the village.

The steady incursion of Western ways and products into many parts of Papua New Guinea has created a demand for cash. One profit-making activity is to cut and sell timber from island rain forests, a practice that could eventually lead to deforestation and erosion. Here, logs have been stacked in the shallows off New Hanover Island, awaiting pickup by commercial boats.

Our experience has been that governments seldom understand the true value of undeveloped forests and aquatic habitats. Decision makers eager for economic expansion look at a wetlands, for example, and assume it is wasted land that could be drained and developed. In fact, wetlands act as hatcheries enriching marine and freshwater fisheries, provide natural purification systems for waste products drained from surrounding lands, help to catch sediments that might otherwise suffocate offshore reefs, and offer shelter for vast populations of birds and wildlife. Eliminating these free services of nature means lost profits in some sectors of the economy, and replacing them can be prohibitively expensive.

For the villagers of Papua New Guinea, undeveloped forests provide food, fuel, clothing, medicines, building materials, tools and implements, boats, ornaments, and other products. They also provide an invaluable sense of belonging in time and space and a spiritual fulfillment, all without money.

Where the forest has been developed, on the other hand, it provides only money. But the money must be spent to replace the free services eliminated when the forest was cut. The independence once secured by self-sufficiency, ensured by the free goods of the forest, gives way to a new dependency on the outside world, as well as spiritual, economic, and family disorientation.

When efforts to improve a society lead to destruction of the envelope of nature that has long sustained it, the society is not helped but harmed. The only legitimate paths to progress lie in developments that combine economic enhancement with environmental preservation. To think that the two are separate issues is to ignore the human predicament: we lead our lives in a womb of nature, as dependent on the health of the ecosphere around us as an unborn infant on the nurturing systems of its mother's body.

While Papua New Guinea's living resources are its most visible assets, the dazzling wealth that has transformed the nation's modest dreams for the future into visions of splendor lies underground. Eons of volcanic uplift have laced some of the country's mountains and islands with vast pockets of precious metals, predominately copper and gold. The discovery of the Panguma copper deposit on Bougainville Island, visited early in the expedition by *Calypso*, inspired mineral exploration in other parts of the country. Within the past few years, this prospecting has revealed unexpected mineral riches of enormous proportion.

The tantalizing possibility, emblazoned daily in the newspapers of the major cities, is that Papua New Guinea could soon become one of the richest countries in the South Pacific. It is believed, for example, that two of the three largest gold deposits in the world are here and that when gold mining is fully developed within the next decade, Papua New Guinea could become the third largest gold producer in the world after South Africa and the Soviet Union.

During the month the Cousteau team had begun to assemble in Port Moresby to prepare the expedition, an alluvial deposit of gold is discovered at Mount Kare, only thirty miles southwest of Porgera. The location is an uninhabited tableland, used only as a hunting grounds by two local clans. The company holding the mining lease decides to keep the find secret until they can organize its recovery. Somehow, word leaks out, and an unpublicized gold rush begins. Government workers in the province simply quit their jobs and disappear, outfitted with shovels and goldpans. Foreigners from Australia and Asia begin to arrive, chartering helicopters so they can slip in, pan a few bags of gold, and slip out.

Ironically, the world outside learns of the gold rush through beer sales in nearby Mount Hagen. Suddenly the orders for beer skyrocket, and distributors are baffled. Where have all these drinkers come from? they wonder. And how can they afford so much beer?

When the public realizes there is accessible gold at Mount Kare, the number of miners swells. Within two months there are a thousand people panning area streams, many of them reportedly making $1,000 a day. Government investigators believe that the foreign miners leaving with suitcases of gold might be illegally carrying off as much as $200,000 a week. With their newfound riches in hand, local villagers walk into Mount Hagen to buy radios, clothing, even automobiles. In two cases, miners purchase cars without any knowledge of how to drive, and promptly wreck them before they can get out of town.

Unknown when the Cousteau team arrives, the Mount Kare gold rush is a national event by the time they leave, illustrating the boom mentality and sudden changes resounding through Papua New Guinea.

Perhaps the most famous and largest mining project in the South Pacific, however, is located at a nearly inaccessible site in the Star Mountains, only ten miles from the country's western border with Irian Jaya. In Papua New Guinea, the words "Ok Tedi" have come to mean both fabulous riches and exasperating headaches. Ok Tedi is essentially a mountain of copper covered by a cap of gold. To dig down to the 376-million-ton reserve of copper, the mine's developers were faced with the enviable problem of first removing the treasury of gold that blocked it, a deposit so large that Ok Tedi soon became the largest gold mine outside South Africa.

The plan that evolved would cover thirty years: five years to extract the gold (a phase now completed), five years to withdraw a mix of gold and copper, and twenty years to remove the copper deposit. Logistics were formidable. A prefabricated town had to be built for 5,000 workers in a roadless mountain jungle. Nearly every scrap of material had to be flown in by helicopters. Nevertheless, the profits were of such magnitude that the mining consortium of Papua New Guinean, Australian, American, and German companies began construction in 1981, with the blessing of the government.

Within three years, problems began to hamper the operation. A fifty-million-ton landslide on the Ok Ma River destroyed the permanent tailings dam designed to capture the mine's massive waste load. Fearful of losing what many projected as the cornerstone of Papua New Guinea's future economy, the government permitted the mine to continue operation without the tailings dam—despite a threat of significant pollution to the Fly River, the country's largest waterway and a source of water and food for some 40,000 villagers.

Six months later, a mine barge overturned, dropping 2,700 drums of cyanide into the Fly estuary. It was the largest release of cyanide into the environment in history. Only 117 drums could be salvaged. Five days later, an accidental dumping of 1,300 cubic yards of highly concentrated cyanide into the Fly River killed fish, prawns, turtles, and crocodiles far downstream from the mine site.

For all the national interest in Ok Tedi, Mount Kare, Porgera, and Misima Island, the largest gold reserve of all in Papua New Guinea may lie on a tiny island off the north coast of New Ireland. The mammoth gold deposit newly discovered at Lihir Island, where people still grow yams and fish for sharks, may amount to 30 million ounces, making it one-third as large as South Africa's largest gold mine and perhaps as great, by itself, as the known gold resources of Australia, the world's fourth largest gold producer. Now undergoing feasibility studies, the Lihir cache of gold has sent shockwaves through the international gold industry.

Despite the dreams of unimaginable wealth sweeping much of Papua New Guinea, the Cousteau team finds in its travels that a powerful environmental ethic still pervades much of the country, the result of centuries of conservation methods practiced from village to village.

To learn more about the traditional attitudes of villagers toward their forests and seas, Dick Murphy visits Dr. John Waiko, Director of the Institute of Applied Social and Economic Research in Port Moresby. Waiko explains that while Western societies have generally viewed nature as an infinite resource to be exploited by humanity without restraint, Papua New Guinea's traditional cultures have believed that nature is limited and that humans must obey rules in order to maintain its balances.

The ancient view of nature arose from spiritual beliefs that in the phenomena of nature—trees, plants, birds, fish, animals—were the origins of human beings; that in some cases these things still housed the spirits of the ancestors, and that villagers had a moral obligation not to cause harm or suffering to them. In the worldview passed down from generation to generation, there was no Creator who provided nature's bounty as a vast gift for human use, and gave humanity dominion over the earth. Nature was an indivisible whole in which human beings were inextricably embedded.

Waiko comes from the Binandere people, who live along the east coast of Papua New Guinea's mainland, to the north of Milne Bay. In 1973, the Binandere were asked by the government and foreign investors to sell their forest rights. Waiko, who was a university student at the time, uses the story of his own people's experiences to illustrate the clash of Western and Papua New Guinean attitudes.

The Binandere were led to believe, he tells Murphy, that the intended project would merely cut trees to build a road, which they welcomed. The money they were offered would help the villagers pay taxes, school fees, and medical expenses. But gradually, the truth emerged. The project would result in clearcutting of the forest, a new town would be built on land traditionally used for gardens, and the result would be that the compensation payments would be spent to buy food the villagers could no longer produce for themselves.

Waiko quotes the response of a village "big man" named Jigede, who voiced the astonishment and anger of the Binandere:

Now I know that the Company intends to clear-cut my forest. Trees do not grow in the air, but on the land. The forest is a source of my medicines, my wealth, my everything. Our ancestors own the place and we have the hunting rights. Not only will the ancestors curse me for accepting a few dollars in exchange for the irreplaceable resource, but also the younger generations will condemn me for my decision to invite the Company. Ancestors have lived here, I am living on the same land, and I want the future generations to have good gardening land. I do not want the Company.

If it ignores my words, say to it that Jigede has said so, and if it ignores again I will impose this condition: that the Company must pay me, my wife, and each member of the family and the extended family a sum of $1,000 every day forever. . . . My children and my children's children must get this sum daily in order to live. These sums added together are nowhere near the price for my land and forest. If the Company is mean and does not want to give this token gesture for destroying my livelihood, not only mine and my family's but that of every single person in the village, warn the Company to forget about my trees on the land.

Waiko tells Murphy that Binandere conservation customs are passed down as part of the oral tradition. One chant portrays a hero named Dungabae, who may have lived in the first half of the nineteenth century and from whom the Binandere learn to revere their surroundings. In an article written by Waiko and another Binandere, Kipling Jiregari, the great ancestor comes to life:

Dungabae quarreled with anyone who trod carelessly in the hunting land and forest and his angry shouts chased the animals away. If he found any sign of footprints he would raise his voice high in the forest and come to the village quarreling and challenging. Dungabae disliked indiscriminate picking of wild fruits and edible leaves, ripe or green. He protested against wastage and the harmful effects of his clansfolk on the wild animals, trees, fruits, even the soil, and indeed, total nature. Dungabae maintained that plants, animals, and the soil had senses or feelings. Accordingly nature felt the pain inflicted upon it by humans, but the soil and the trees had no mouth to scream protest. Therefore, Dungabae was their mouth to quarrel with anyone who picked unripe fruits, cut trees, and even notched plants wantonly and disturbed the environment unnecessarily. In brief, Dungabae protected the rights of nature and stood for the "mouthless." He was nature's man.

A common sight among Papua New Guinea's 600 offshore islands is families routinely traveling to visit friends or clan members in homemade canoes. The fact that villagers venture confidently on the high seas in tiny boats with their children aboard attests to their thorough understanding of the sea and sailing, a body of knowledge passed down across thousands of years.

Waiko tells Murphy that despite the success of his people in resisting the loss of their forests, he is pessimistic about the future. The pressures from outside the community, from the national government, and foreign entrepreneurs is so great that ultimately it will lead to the destruction of the forests. He has decided to try to preserve on film the customs, dances, and oral traditions of the Binandere for future generations in case the next battles, sure to come, are lost.

On June 19th, after finally succeeding in their attempts to film shark calling on New Ireland Island, the crew of *Alcyone* sets out on a westward course across the Bismarck Sea. Two days later the ship reaches Manus Island, where the team finds a traditional method of harvesting the sea that bears resemblance to the forest conservation practices of the Binandere and other inland peoples.

At tiny A'hus Island off the north coast of Manus, the team is shown "clam gardens" along a shallow reef. According to ancient traditions, families and clan groups are considered reef keepers: each is assigned ownership of portions of the offshore area, where they can harvest only what they consume. Each clan group has its own fishing methods, a custom that acts to limit the pressures on any one species, and they follow time-honored practices that help to ensure the vitality of their waters. It is known, for example, where coral trout (groupers) congregate for mass reproduction, and though villagers harvest the fish, they wait until after spawning is completed and the fish are leaving the reproduction site.

Diving to inspect the clam gardens, the Cousteau team finds giant tridacnas arrayed in shallow underwater pens walled with empty shells. They count as many as thirty clams per garden and estimate that some

A Cousteau diver inspects a "garden" of giant *Tridacna* clams at A'hus Island near Manus. Families raise the clams, some of which grow to 500 pounds, in shallow pens. Local custom assigns "ownership" of portions of the reef to village clans, who are considered "keepers" of their seabottom territory.

weigh as much as 400 to 500 pounds. For generations, families have tended to their watery gardens and fished only within their assigned reef boundaries, moving from place to place within their territories to enable the regrowth of new generations of fish, as forest peoples leave land fallow so that it will regenerate fertility.

In a meeting with Manus Premier Stephen Pokawin, however, Dick Murphy learns that the ancient system is breaking down. With the intrusion of a new cash economy, villagers often overharvest their reefs, catching more than they can eat and selling the surplus to raise money. Many people on Manus now earn cash by free diving extensively for *Trochus* shells, which are exported to Japan for the manufacture of buttons.

As the economic value of these ocean resources increases, Pokawin tell Murphy, so does the temptation to fish in someone else's backyard. Fistfights and feuds are becoming commonplace, and the social conflicts are further exacerbated by the gradual depletion of fish and *Trochus* shells, fueling the pressures to trespass.

Murphy asks why villagers are driven so intensely to accumulate money? There are a variety of reasons. Education is not free, forcing families to turn their resources into cash to send their children to school. Traditional feasts and gift giving—now involving the purchase of foods and manufactured products—has become an expensive custom. As marine sources of food decline with the overfishing, families grow more dependent on the purchase of "tin fish" from markets.

The escalating demand for money has encouraged young people to leave Manus to find jobs in distant towns so they can send money back to their families. The money earners grow weary of working constantly to support their entire clan, some of whom take advantage of the situation and lead idle lives.

There are two more problems, Pokawin says, which are adding to the complexity of their resource-management dilemma. Foreign fishing boats, many from Taiwan, are also entering Manus waters, enraging local people. Such fishing is nearly impossible to monitor, and the islanders have no effective fleet to intercept the foreigners. Another problem is that undetonated explosives from World War II can still be found on Manus, which was a large Allied base. The competition for ocean resources has driven some of the local people to catch fish by using these explosives to blow up reefs, causing great harm.

Manus islander Job Kilangit displays abandoned ammunition he found in forests on the island, where a huge Allied base was camped during World War II. Old undetonated explosives are used by some fishermen, who destroy large areas of reefs when "dynamiting" fish. Kilangit lost a hand while using such explosives.

Left: A Cousteau
team cameraman
approaches two orcas
off Wuvulu Island in
the Bismarck Sea. On
other occasions, orcas
encountered in the
wild have departed
when the divers
entered the water.
Here, a total of three
orcas lingered,
seemingly oblivious to
the visitors.

Following pages:
A sight perhaps never
before witnessed in
the wild by humans:
two orcas filmed near
Wuvulu Island play
with the remains of a
shark they have
captured and torn
apart. Perhaps in fear
of the whales, local
reef sharks had fled to
the deep from these
predators, which some
believe to be the
mightiest and most
intelligent hunters in
the sea. The orcas
dove into the depths
and returned with
their prey. To the
astonishment of the
Cousteau team, the
whales paraded their
catch before the divers
then shook it violently
like playful dogs
before finally
consuming the lifeless
pieces. The whales
could have gone
anywhere to feed on
the shark yet returned
to the site where
divers waited.

J.-M. C.: On June 24th, I return to Alcyone with my son Fabien for our last mission in Papua New Guinea. Mike Sullivan flies us in Papagallo to the Hermit Islands, where the windship has been anchored for two days. When we have climbed aboard, I call a crew meeting to discuss my plans for the coming week. For me, the last leg of our expedition amounts to a sentimental journey, a return to the island of Wuvulu, where I first became enchanted with Papua New Guinea fifteen years ago, and where I first dreamed of bringing my father and our crews for a major expedition.

Two days later, the low profile of Wuvulu appears on the horizon ahead. As we arrive offshore, canoes surround us immediately. From the deck I see friends from my previous visits, and at my prompting they scramble aboard, surprised to see a familiar face on this strange-looking white vessel. I take them on a tour of Alcyone, pleased to be able to extend hospitality to villagers who have welcomed me into their homes and councils over the years. We share some memories in the carré, talk about mutual friends from my world and theirs, and make plans to meet later on the island.

When they depart, the team and I organize a dive immediately. I am anxious to see if Wuvulu's reefs are as beautiful as I remember, and the team is curious about an undersea realm that has evoked such superlatives from me.

They are captivated, too, within moments of our entering the water, for the colors are vibrant, the fish dazzling. We explore caves, glide alongside groupers, hang entranced to contemplate the intricate patterns of corals and crinoids, sponges, and starfish.

Yet as we share our impressions of the reef while climbing out of our suits, I realize that something was missing. On other dives I had made at this site off Wuvulu, sharks commonly roamed the reefs. Today, I hadn't seen a single one. I wondered if something unusual was going on and resolved to search further for sharks on upcoming dives.

That evening, as we sit with the villagers, I mention our puzzlement at the lack of sharks on the reef. "The sharks are all in hiding," says one islander, "because the whales are here now." As if on cue, someone in the village suddenly shouts, "The whales!", pointing just beyond the reef.

David Brown, Fabien, and I jump into the Zodiac to have a look. As we pass the edge of the reef, an orca surfaces only yards away, as if inspecting us, then slips directly beneath the Zodiac. Although we have filmed orcas elsewhere, most recently in the waters of British Columbia, our encounters with these supreme predators of the sea have always been frustrating. Despite their innate superiority in the medium of water, the whales seem reluctant to approach our cameras. It has thus been difficult to capture sharp images of the creatures through the cold, murky waters of the northern Pacific.

Watching this curious whale disappear below our Zodiac into the clear waters of Wuvulu, I wonder if it might be possible to obtain here the orca footage we have always sought. I have no way of knowing the extraordinary encounters in store for us.

It is raining the next morning, but we decide to start the day by exploring fully some underwater caves only glimpsed during our first dive at Wuvulu. As we approach the dive site in a Zodiac, I see movement near the surface of the water, then the unmistakable bulbous snouts of two orcas. It is as if they are waiting for our arrival. Soon a third whale joins the others, and the trio swims about slowly, giving us the impression they are not ready to take flight. I suspect that one is a young male, perhaps accompanied by two females.

We enter the water immediately, fearful of losing this rare opportunity to catch a few frames of orcas in clear water. Prezelin and I move slowly toward the whales, uncertain what to expect, almost disbelieving that this unexpected moment is taking place, trying to ignore the fact that we are approaching creatures whose ability to attack and consume prey surpasses even the greatest of sharks.

When we are within twenty feet of the orcas, I notice that there is something odd about the shape of the male's mouth. At first sight, it looks as if the jaws are grotesquely malformed or damaged. I wonder if it has been injured. We try to approach closer, and the creature swims away, then makes a pass near us from right to left. Suddenly Louis and I look at one another, astonished to realize that we are swimming among, and Louis is filming, orcas in the midst of a hunt. The curious mouth of the male is not misshapen at all. Clenched tightly in its mighty jaws is a seven-foot manta ray.

My mind reels. I try to recall if such orca behavior has ever been witnessed in the wild, if it has ever been documented on film. I decide it has probably not, but that this is no time to let my mind wander. Before us, the great hunter swims back and forth, as if proud and anxious to parade its catch before Louis's camera. Then, as we draw a little closer, the orca begins to shake the manta violently. I think of a cat playing with a captured mouse, yet this is play of another order. Chunks of the manta's entrails hang in the water like frozen fragments from an explosion. A cloud of blood billows from the dead creature. A piece of its winglike fins breaks off and settles toward the bottom.

Now the orca releases the manta and the carcass begins to sink. We can see teethmarks in the body and huge chunks of flesh torn away. Looking down, I realize that we are in water perhaps several hundred feet deep, beyond the steep dropoff of the reef. We peer into a blue infinity. As the manta settles into this oblivion, the orca suddenly returns, swooping down to catch it. Louis and I are now about a hundred feet deep, and the whale is another fifty feet below us. With the manta wedged in its mouth, the creature rolls over on its back, revealing a white patch on its belly. The furious shaking and whipping of the dead prey begins again. Eventually, there is little remaining of the manta. What has not been eaten has been torn apart and left to the currents and the bottom. Hours later, before our cameras, the orcas similarly toy with and devour a shark captured in the depths.

For all the startling violence, there is a riveting finality and a cold beauty to the scene before us. We are privileged witnesses to a moment of survival and slaughter in the lawless ranges of the sea. Energy and matter pass from one creature to another, and despite the enormity and power of the spectacle, it has no more significance in the grand scheme of nature than the consumption of an anchovy by a sea gull. Life is lost. Life is sustained.

We are spellbound. Slipping back into the Zodiac we burst into howls of joy, shaking our heads at such great fortune, to have happened upon a scene that divers only dream about; literally rendered speechless by the magnitude of the experience. We are probably the first human beings in history to have witnessed the sea's greatest hunter at its moment of conquest in the wild.

We return to Alcyone, exhausted, exhilarated, benumbed by the day's surprises, awestruck by the visions etched forever in our memories. I ask Alain Furic to open a bottle of champagne, and we settle around the table in the carré sharing our thoughts until weariness and watch duties draw an end to the day.

Lying in my bunk, unable to sleep, I reflect on the unpredictable nature of our work. After the months of planning, the seemingly endless days our crews spent carrying out tedious and tiring duties, the frustrations of our logistics people in dealing with bureaucratic complexities, the punishing travel, the disappointments when stories didn't pan out or dives revealed little, the stuck anchor chain, the malfunctioning communications system and air conditioning, the stolen equipment, the rains and muddy roads, the heat, humidity, ear infec-

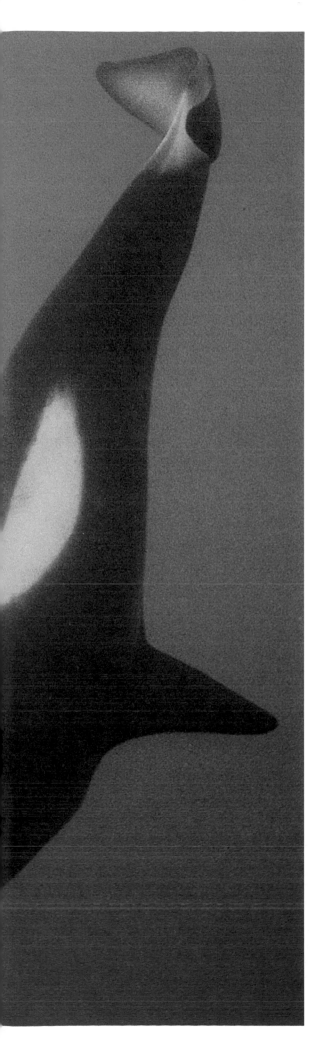

tions, and mosquitoes—after all of this marathon of endurance for our teams, an unexpected encounter in the sea suddenly transports us into a world where few humans have ever been, reveals scenes no human has ever watched, provides us with film images that will entrance millions of viewers and enhance our understanding of life and death in the world ocean. All of this during eight hours on one of the last days of the expedition. All of this resulting from an event our researchers could not have foreseen, generated by creatures we did not even expect to come upon. Somehow, the hardships that covered months seem trivial compared to the magic of this one day.

I think of our deliberations over the nature of "happiness" and realize that, although I cannot define it nor arrive at a formula for it, my comrades on Alcyone and I will undoubtedly long recall this day as one of supreme happiness, merging all of the joys we share—the sea, the observation of earth's untamed creatures, the sensual pleasure of gliding weightlessly through a liquid sky, the discovery of previously unseen events, the feeling of being at the edge of danger yet under control, the enchantment of living an unpredictable existence. Every human could arrive at such a list, and the pleasures would be as diverse as our species, yet my experiences are that some joys are universal. The moment of enrichment as new knowledge surges into the mind, the wonder at nature's awesome spectacles, the sensual delights of our physical being, the beauty of color and water and light and living forms, all seem to me sources of pleasure that lighten the burdens and bring smiles to the faces of people everywhere.

Finally, this day of happiness leads me to think about our deliberations over the value of nature. Beyond our biological dependence on a healthy environment, there may be an equally important service it renders to humans, and that is nature's infinite capacity to inspire us. It is no wonder that the peoples of Papua New Guinea have long celebrated and protected animals and plants, fish and trees, as repositories of the spirits. There is nothing we humans have yet invented or imagined to compare with the artwork, the organizational complexity, or the power and resilience of nature.

Our dream for Papua New Guinea is that the spiritual sustenance its people derive from their beautiful forests and seas never be lost as the nation rushes into the future. It is important to educate young minds and to ensure the health of young bodies and to lessen hardships with appropriate new technologies, but it is also important to safeguard far into the future the gifts of nature in Papua New Guinea that inspire the human heart—forests adorned with hibiscus and orchid and bird of paradise, rivers alive with mangrove and cassowary and crocodile, seas abounding with coral and giant clam and shark, and with whales that play like lions in the jungle of the sea.

As we leave Papua New Guinea, these wonders endure, and if the ancient reverence for nature guides those crafting the future, this luxuriant realm born of volcanoes and tropical fecundity can still be saved, can serve as a model for other nations, can survive as a source of inspiration and wisdom for all the world.

INDEX

PHOTOGRAPH CREDITS

Patrick Allioux: *1*; David Brown: *5, 173, 213, 216*; Anne-Marie Cousteau: *8–9, 10–11, 12, 16, 19, 27, 28, 30, 49, 74, 77* (top), *78, 80, 81, 82, 83* (both), *84, 85, 86, 87, 89, 90, 91, 92, 93, 94–95, 96, 97, 99, 100, 101* (both), *102, 104–105, 119, 124, 130, 132, 133, 134–135, 136, 137, 139, 140, 141* (all), *142* (both), *143, 145, 146* (both), *147, 148* (both), *149, 150, 151* (both), *152, 154, 155, 156, 182, 190–191, 208*; Chuck Davis: *22* (both), *167, 218–219*; Richard C. Murphy: *18, 26, 29* (both), *41, 76, 162–163* (all), *164* (top), *193, 196, 200, 204, 215*; Didier Noirot: *2–3, 4, 6–7, 24, 31, 32, 34, 35, 36* (both), *37, 38–39, 42–43* (all), *45, 46–47* (both), *52, 54–55, 56, 57, 58* (both), *59, 60, 61* (both), *62, 64, 67, 68, 69, 70, 72, 73, 106, 110, 111, 112, 116–117, 118, 120–121. 122, 123, 125, 126, 127, 128–129, 158–159, 160* (both), *161, 164* (middle and bottom), *165, 166–167, 175, 176, 177* (both), *178, 179, 180–181, 186, 187, 194, 195, 197, 198–199, 203, 209*; Mose Richards: *174*; Clay Wilcox: *201, 220–221*; Map on pages *14–15* by Paul Pugliese.

ACKNOWLEDGMENTS

We would like to thank Karen Brazeau and Dr. Richard C. Murphy, whose hard work under difficult circumstances made this expedition possible and successful, and Neal Shapiro, whose research helped shape the expedition and the book. Thanks also to team members who aided in the making of this book by recording written and audio journals of their experiences in Papua New Guinea: Dick Murphy, Anne-Marie Cousteau, Yves Zlotnicka, Jean-Paul Cornu, and Steve Arrington. Many new friends in Papua New Guinea made generous contributions to the expedition, for which we offer our sincere gratitude: Peter Barter, Keli and Joan Taureka, Bob, Dinah, and Telita Halstead, Ian Chapman, Ron and Ronnie Knight, Kukura Tibong, Michael Boagin, John Waiko, Max Benjamin, John McCloud, Bill Rudd, Jerome Koubuli, Ivan Huasi, Goetz Von Schwenfurth, Clem Leahy, the staff of the Islander Hotel, and the people of Komuniva, Kindau, Wasaami, Boga Boga, Chambri Lake, Korogo, Kubkain, Timbunke, Kambaramba, Goodenough Island, Fergusson Island, Iwa Island, Wuvulu Island, and the Hermit Islands.